CHORE CHART
&
ALLOWANCE BOOK
For Kids

お小遣い帳　小学生

52 Weekly Money Log: Empowering Kids to

Manage Money and Achieve Goals

子供達にお金の管理と目標達成の力を

教える 52 週間マネーログ

BILINGUAL LEARNINGS

This
CHORE CHART & ALLOWANCE BOOK
belongs to:

_____

このお小遣い帳は

_____

のものです。

Table of Contents 目次

INTRODUCTION

Welcome to the weekly Chore Chart & Allowance Book! Thank you for choosing this book to help you manage and improve your money skills. Do you ever find yourself wondering if you have enough money for something you want to buy? This book is designed to help you answer that question, and much more!

As Peter Drucker said, "You can't manage what you can't measure." This means that in order to manage your money well, you need to be able to measure it. With this workbook, you will be able to visually measure your progress toward your financial goals and know exactly how much you have to spend.

It's also important to note that "if you can't measure it, you can't improve it" by Peter Drucker. By tracking your finances on a weekly basis, you'll not only be able to manage your money more effectively, but you'll also be able to identify areas for improvement and make progress toward your financial goals.

This workbook will help you establish healthy money habits and relationships by encouraging you to quantify, measure, reflect, and adjust your progress and processes on a weekly basis. As you work through the pages, you'll set

はじめに

ようこそ！この小学生の為のお小遣い帳をご購入頂きありがとうございます。自分が欲しいものを買うために十分なお金があるかどうか、疑問に思ったことはありませんか？この本はあなたがその質問に答えられる様、さらに多くのことが出来る手助けになるように作られました。

ピータードラッカーが言ったように、「計測出来ないものを管理できない」です。つまり、お金を上手に管理するためには、それを測定できるひつようがあります。このワークブックでは、視覚的にあなたの財政目標にむけた進捗状況を計測し、どのくらい使えるお金があるかを正確に把握することができます。

また、ピータードラッカーが言ったように、「計測出来ないものは改善できない」ということも重要です。毎週、週単位であなたの財政を追跡することによって、あなたはあなたのお金をより効果的に管理することができるだけでなく、あなたはまた改善すべき領域を特定し、そして。あなたの財政目標に向かって進歩することができます。

このワークブックは、週ごとの進捗状況やプロセスの数量化、計測、反映、調整を促すため、健康的なお金の習慣や関係を確立するのに訳立ちます。ページを進めながら、現実的な

realistic goals, track your chores and allowance, log your earnings and spendings and celebrate your wins!

By the end of the book, you'll be more in control of your finances and have a better understanding of your money habits. So, let's get started on your journey to financial success!

If you enjoy this workbook, please visit www.bilinguallearnings.com and sign up for our newsletters for more fun workbooks, books, resources, tips and strategies that help parents, who are raising Japanese/English bilingual kids or older kids/adults, who want to keep up with their Japanese/English bilingual level and skills with fun!

目標を設定し、家事とお小遣いを把握し、収入と支出を記録し、自分の成果を祝福することができます。

本の終わりには、あなたは自分の財政をよりコントロールでき、自分のお金の習慣をよりよく理解できるようになってるでしょう。それでは、あなたの財政成功への旅を始めましょう!

もし、このワークブックを楽しんで頂けましたら、是非、www.bilinguallearnings.com にて、ニュースレターに登録してください。日英バイリンガルの子供を育てている親や、日英バイリンガルのレベルやスキルを、楽しみながら、維持していきたいと感じている若者や大人達の為に、もっと楽しいワークブック、本、資料や戦略などについて、お送りいたします!

LET'S COUNT! – MONEY USED IN THE USA

1 cent (Penny)	$0.01	1 ¢	
5 cents (Nickel)	$0.05	5 ¢	
10 cents (Dime)	$0.10	10 ¢	
25 cents (Quarter)	$0.25	25 ¢	
1 dollar	$1.00	100 ¢	
2 dollars	$2.00		
5 dollars	$5.00		
10 dollars	$10.00		
20 dollars	$20.00		
100 dollars	$100.00		

数えよう！– 日本で使われているお金

1 えん	一円	￥1	
5 えん	五円	￥5	
10 えん	十円	￥10	
50 えん	五十円	￥50	
100 えん	百円	￥100	
500 えん	五百円	￥500	
1,000 えん	千円	￥1,000	
5,000 えん	五千円	￥5,000	
10,000 えん	一万円	￥10,000	

How to use this chore chart & allowance book

You can start using the Chore Chart & Allowance Book anytime! Simply use the blank lines to note the dates and week. We recommend choosing a consistent day of the week that works for you to take 10-15 minutes to set goals, note results and celebrate wins. Sundays work well for us to review the previous week's progress and set goals for the new week, but it can be any day that you can commit to consistently!

THE WEEKLY PROCESS

1) Choose up to 5 chores to work on a week

Think about and list up chores or other works that you would like to challenge. Discuss them with your parents. If you can't come up with any chores or other tasks, ask your parents for any suggestions. Here are some suggestions for chores:

For young kids: putting away toys and books, feeding pets, dusting furniture, making their bed, sweeping small areas with a broom or dustpan, setting the table for meals, cleaning the table after meals, wiping down kitchen counters or cabinets, watering plants, sorting laundry by separating lights and dark colors.

このお小遣い帳の使い方

このお小遣い帳はいつでも使い始めることができます！空白に日付と週を記入しましょう。毎週10〜15分、目標を設定し、結果を記録し、勝利を祝うことができる、一貫した曜日を選択することをお勧めします。日曜日は、前週の進捗状況を確認し、新しい週の目標を設定するのに適していますが、一貫してコミットできる日であればいつでも大丈夫です。

週ごとのプロセス

1) その週にやるお手伝いを 1〜5 つまで選択しよう。

挑戦したい家事や他のお手伝いを考え、書き留めましょう。内容を両親と一緒に話し合ってみましょう。もし、家事や他のお手伝いが思いつかない場合は、両親に提案してもらいましょう。以下はお手伝いのアイディアです。

小学生低学年：
おもちゃや本を片付ける、ペットに餌をやる、家具のほこりとり、ベッドを整える、ほうきやちりとりで小さな場所を掃く、食事のためのテーブルセットする、食後のテーブルを拭く、キッチンカウンターやキャビネットを拭く、植物に水をやる、洗濯物を明るい色と暗い色に分ける、など。

For older kids: washing dishes, loading and unloading the dishwasher, vacuuming floors or carpets, Mowing the lawn, taking out the trash and recycling, folding and putting away laundry, washing the car, clearing bathrooms, cooking simple meals with supervision.

2) Set your weekly goals

Note your wish list items and prices. Then, decide and write how many chores you would like to mark as complete and achieve for the week. Having a target to work towards can help motivate you and make it easier to track your progress.

Setting goals is important because it helps you clarify what you want to achieve and provides a roadmap to get there. When you have clear goals in mind, you are more likely to take action and make progress towards achieving them. Goals also give you direction, motivation, and a sense of purpose.

In terms of managing money, setting financial goals can help you prioritize your spending and savings, and make decisions that align with your long-term aspirations. It can also help you avoid impulsive purchases or overspending. By setting achievable goals and tracking your progress, you can stay on track and celebrate your successes along the way!

小学生高学年：

皿洗い、食器洗い機の積み下ろし、床やカーペットの掃除機かけ、芝刈り、ゴミとリサイクルのゴミ出し、洗濯物をたたんでしまう、車を洗う、バスルームの掃除、監視の下で簡単な食事をつくる、など。

2）その週の目標を設定しよう。

あなたのほしいもののリストと価格を書き留めましょう。次に、その週に完了して達成したいお手伝いの数を決定し、書き留めましょう。向かっていく目標があることは、あなたのやる気を起こさせ、進捗状況を追跡しやすくするのに役立ちます。

目標を設定することは、達成したいことを明確にし、そこに到達するための道筋を提供するのに役立つため、重要です。明確な目標を持っていると、行動を起こし、その達成に向けて前進することがより可能になります。目標はまた、あなたに方向性、モチベーション、そして目的意識を与えてくれます。

お金の管理に関しては、財務目標を設定することで、支出や貯蓄に優先順位を付け、長期的な希望に合わせた決定をすることができます。また、衝動買いや過剰な支出を避けるのにも役立ちます。達成可能な目標を設定し、進捗状況を追跡することで、自分が納得いく方向に進み、成功を祝うことができます!

3) Track your progress everyday

Mark your chores as complete or incomplete for each day. Log any events with receiving and spending money for that day. In Illustration pages, you can find some guidance on how to track events related to receiving and spending money, such as "received $1 for doing extra chores" and "spent $3 on a snack."

4) Review

Write the total number of chores marked complete, compare it against your goal, and investigate the reasons for the difference to:

a) Identify areas for improvement:
By investigating why the goal was not met, you can identify any obstacles you need to overcome in order to achieve your goals and any areas where improvement is needed. This can help you adjust your approach to make it more effective and efficient.

b) Learn from mistakes:
Understanding why you didn't meet your goal can help you learn from your mistakes and avoid making the same mistakes in the future.

c) Keep motivated:
When you know why you didn't meet your goal, you can use this information to stay motivated and focused on achieving your next goal.

3）毎日、進捗を記録しよう

毎日のお手伝いについて、完了または未完了として印をつけましょう。その日のお金の受け取りと支出に関するイベントを記録しましょう。イラストのページにて、「追加のお手伝いをすることで1ドルを受け取った」や「おやつに3ドルを使った」など、お金の受け取りや支出に関するイベントの追跡方法のガイダンスが載っています。

4）レビューをしよう

完了と印されたお手伝いの合計を書き込み、それを目標と比較し、下記の目的を考慮しながら、違いの理由を調べてみましょう。

ア）改善すべき箇所を特定する:
目標が達成されなかった理由を調べることで、目標を達成するために克服しなければならない障害や改善が必要な箇所を特定することができます。これにより、自分のアプローチをより効果的かつ効率的に調整するのに役立ちます。

イ）失敗から学ぶ:
目標を達成できなかった理由を理解することで、自分の失敗から学び、将来同じ失敗を繰り返さないようにするのに役立ちます。

ウ）やる気を維持する:
目標を達成できなかった理由を知っていれば、その情報を利用しながら、次の目標を達成するためのモチベーションを維持し、集中することができます。

d) Make adjustments:

Investigating the reasons for any differences between the total number of chores completed and the goal can help you make adjustments to your approach or your goals. You may need to adjust your expectations or change your strategy to be more successful in the future.

e) Celebrate successes:

By understanding why you met your goal, you can celebrate your successes and use this positive feedback to motivate yourself to continue working toward your goals.

Also, note any extra tasks completed for that week. Copy the "ending balance" from previous week to "starting balance" of the current week. Calculate and write down the ending balance for the current week.

5) Celebrate

Note any wins for the week! Be proud of your accomplishments, efforts and progress. Even a little progress can lead to a big result with consistency. You are doing great! Here are some of examples of wins that you might celebrate:

1-Completing all chores for the week
2-Meeting or exceeding their weekly chore completion goal
3-Making progress towards a larger savings goal
4-Saving up enough money to buy a wish list item you've been wanting
5-Demonstrating improved responsibility and organization skills

エ）調整を行う：

完了したお手伝いの合計と目標の違いの理由を調べることで、自分のアプローチや目標を調整するのに役立ちます。将来、より成功するためには、期待値や予測を調整したり、戦略をかえたりする必要があるかもしれません。

オ）成功を祝う：

目標を達成した理由を理解することで、成功を祝い、そのポジティブなフィードバックを使って、目標に向かって取り組み続けるように自分自身をモチベートすることができます。

また、その週に完了した追加のお手伝いも記録しましょう。前週の「のこったおかね」を今週の「はじまのおかね」にうつしましょう。今週の「のこったおかね」を計算して書き留めましょう。

5）お祝いしよう

今週の成果を記録しましょう！自分の成果、努力、進歩に誇りをもちましょう。小さな進歩だけでも、一貫して取り組めば、大きな結果につながります。あなたは素晴らしいことをしています！　以下は、あなたにお祝してほしい、いくつかの勝利の例です：

1-その週のすべてのお手伝いを完了できた。
2-その週の達成したいお手伝いの目標を満たすか、超えた。
3-より大きな貯金の目標に向けて前に進んだ。
4-欲しいものリストにある商品を買うために十分な、お金を貯めた。
5-責任感と管理する能力を向上させたことを証明することができた。

6-Consistently tracking your progress and staying committed to the process
7-Earning additional rewards or bonuses for going above and beyond expectations
8-Learning how to effectively budget your allowance and manage your spending habits
9-Feeling a sense of accomplishment and pride for taking ownership of your responsibilities
10-Developing a strong work ethic and sense of discipline
11-Gaining more confidence and independence in managing your finances
12-Improving your communication and negotiation skills when discussing chores and allowance with their parents.

6) Reflect and Adjust

Compare your ending balance to your wish list. If you didn't achieve your goal, take some time to think about why and brainstorm strategies for doing better next week. Consider any unexpected events or circumstances that might have impacted your progress. Some examples of adjustments include changing your goal to a more realistic and achievable one, choosing different chores to work on, or adjusting your allowance.

Once you've made any necessary adjustments, decide on which chores to keep, add, or remove for the following week. You might want to consider which chores were the most enjoyable or challenging and adjust accordingly. Note these decisions on a new page and then go back to step 1 to repeat the process for a new week.

6- 進捗状況を一貫して記録し、プロセスにコミットし続けた。

7-期待を超えることで、追加のおこづかい、またはボーナスをもらった。

8-お小遣いを効果的に予算し、支出習慣を管理する方法を学んだ。

9-責任を持ってやりとげたことに対して達成感と誇りを感じた。

10-強い労働倫理と自己規律を身につけた。

11-お金の管理について、自信と独立性をより高めた。

12-お手伝いやお小遣いについて両親と話し合う際のコミュニケーションと交渉スキルを向上させた。

6) 反映して調整しよう

のこったおかねを欲しいものリストとくらべてみましょう。目標を達成できなかった場合は、その理由を考え、来週の改善策を考えてみましょう。進歩に影響を与えたかもしれない予期せぬ出来事や状況も考慮してみましょう。調整の例としては、目標をより現実的で達成可能なものに変更する、別のお手伝いを選択する、お小遣い額を調整するなどが含まれます。

必要な調整ができたら、翌週に追加するお手伝い、維持するお手伝い、削除するお手伝いを決定しましょう。どのお手伝いが最も楽しかったか、またはチャレンジングだったかも考えて、調整しましょう。これらの決定を新しいページに記録し、新しい週のプロセスを繰り返すために、上記のステップ1に戻りましょう。

Week of / こんしゅうのひづけ _____ 4/16/2023 _____

| Goals for this week
こんしゅうのもくひょう | ☆ Chores to complete
おてつだいをするかいすう _____ 20 _____ | times
かい |
| | ☆ Money to earn:
こんしゅう、うけとりたいおかね _____ $5.00 _____ | |

Chores おてつだいのないよう	S にち	M げつ	T か	W すい	T もく	F きん	S ど
1 一 Wash my plate	✓	✓	✗	✓	✓	✗	✗
2 二 さらあらいをする	●	●	●	●	●	○	●
3 三 Clean play area	○	●	○	●	●	○	●
4 四 おかたづけする	○	●	○	●	●	○	●
5 五 _____	○	○	○	○	○	○	○

> Everyday, mark the circles with check marks and Xs or coloring it with your favorite color!
>
> まいにち、○にチェックやXマークをつけるか、すきないろでぬってみましょう！

| Memo
メモ | I couldn't do any chores on Friday, because I went to a sleepover.
きんようびは、スリープオーバーをしたから、おてつだいできなかった。 |

☆ Results / けっか

This week, I completed chores
こんしゅう、おてつだいができたかいすう _____ 18 _____ times かい

From my chores, I earned
おてつだいをして、うけとったおかね _____ $4.50 _____

From extra work, I earned extra
ついかのおてつだいをして、うけとったおかね _____ $1.00 (Helped pulling out weeds.
くさとりをした。)

☆ Celebrate WINS! / せいかのおいわいをしましょう！

I am proud of myself for
できて、ほこりにおもうこと _____ I got $5.50 in total!
ごうけい$5.50もらった！ _____

I went above and beyond by doing
いつもより、もっとがんばってやりとげたこと _____ Pulling out weeds was hard, but I did it!
くさとりはたいへんだったけど、がんばった！ _____

> Note any wins! Small or big, wins are wins! You are doing great!
>
> どんなせいこうでもかきましょう！ちいさくても、おおきくても、せいこうはせいこうです！あなたはよくやっています！

My wish list ほしいものリスト	I am saving my money for: わたしがおかねをためているりゆう	
	My wish list / ほしいものリスト	Price / きんがく
1 一	Cute notebook　かわいいノート	$ 15.00
2 二	Hello Kitty bag　ハローキティーのバッグ	$20.00
3 三		

Money Log
マネーログ

Note the ending balance from last week.
せんしゅう、のこったおかねをかきましょう。

My wallet
わたしのさいふのなか
Starting balance
はじめのおかね　$34.82

Date 月／日	Description ないよう	Money received はいったおかね	Money spent つかったおかね	Balance のこったおかね
4/16	Extra work ついかのおてつだい	$1.00		35.82
4/18	Snack おやつ		$3.00	32.82
4/22	Allowance おこづかい	$4.50		37.32
4/22	Save in Piggy ちょきんばこにうつす		$5.00	32.32

How much I saved so far / いままでで たまったおかね　$32.82

Check for any difference between the total cash in hand and the calculated ending balance.

My piggy bank savings
わたしのちょきんばこのなか
Starting balance:
はじめのおかね　$25.00

Date 月／日	Description ないよう	Money received はいったおかね	Money spent つかったおかね	Balance のこったおかね
4/22	Save ちょきん	$5.00		130.00

How much I saved so far / いままでで、たまったおかね　$130.00

てもちのおかねのごうけいと、けいさんした、のこりのおかねにちがいがないか、かくにんしましょう。

Note all money activities in this section.
このらんにおかねのうごきをきろくしましょう。

Moving some money to "My Piggy Bank Saving" every week, even a small amount, is a great practice to increase your savings!

まいしゅう、すこしでもちょきんばこにおかねをうつすのは、ちょきんをふやせる、よいしゅうかんです。

15

The Weekly Tracker Pages
(52 weeks)

週ごとのトラッカーページ

（52週間分）

Week of / こんしゅうのひづけ _____

Goals for this week こんしゅうのもくひょう	☆ Chores to complete おてつだいをするかいすう _____	times かい
	☆ Money to earn: こんしゅう、うけとりたいおかね _____	

Chores おてつだいのないよう	S にち	M げつ	T か	W すい	T もく	F きん	S ど
1 一 _____	○	○	○	○	○	○	○
2 二 _____	○	○	○	○	○	○	○
3 三 _____	○	○	○	○	○	○	○
4 四 _____	○	○	○	○	○	○	○
5 五 _____	○	○	○	○	○	○	○

Memo
メモ

☆ Results / けっか

This week, I completed chores   times
こんしゅう、おてつだいができたかいすう _____ かい

From my chores, I earned
おてつだいをして、うけとったおかね _____

From extra work, I earned extra
ついかのおてつだいをして、うけとったおかね _____

☆ Celebrate WINS! / せいかのおいわいをしましょう!

I am proud of myself for
できて、ほこりにおもうこと _____

I went above and beyond by doing
いつもより、もっとがんばってやりとげたこと _____

My wish list ほしいものリスト	I am saving my money for: わたしがおかねをためているりゆう	
	My wish list / ほしいものリスト	Price / きんがく
1 一		
2 二		
3 三		

Money Log
マネーログ

My wallet
わたしのさいふのなか

Starting balance
はじめのおかね _____

Date 月／日	Description ないよう	Money received はいったおかね	Money spent つかったおかね	Balance のこったおかね

How much I saved so far / いままでで、たまったおかね _____

My piggy bank savings
わたしのちょきんばこのなか

Starting balance:
はじめのおかね _____

Date 月／日	Description ないよう	Money received はいったおかね	Money spent つかったおかね	Balance のこったおかね

How much I saved so far / いままでで、たまったおかね _____

Week of / こんしゅうのひづけ _____

| Goals for this week
こんしゅうのもくひょう | ☆ Chores to complete
おてつだいをするかいすう _____ | times
かい |
| | ☆ Money to earn:
こんしゅう、うけとりたいおかね _____ | |

Chores おてつだいのないよう	S にち	M げつ	T か	W すい	T もく	F きん	S ど
1 一 _____	○	○	○	○	○	○	○
2 二 _____	○	○	○	○	○	○	○
3 三 _____	○	○	○	○	○	○	○
4 四 _____	○	○	○	○	○	○	○
5 五 _____	○	○	○	○	○	○	○

| Memo
メモ |
| |

☆ Results / けっか

This week, I completed chores   times
こんしゅう、おてつだいができたかいすう _____ かい

From my chores, I earned
おてつだいをして、うけとったおかね _____

From extra work, I earned extra
ついかのおてつだいをして、うけとったおかね _____

☆ Celebrate WINS! / せいかのおいわいをしましょう!

I am proud of myself for
できて、ほこりにおもうこと _____

I went above and beyond by doing
いつもより、もっとがんばってやりとげたこと _____

My wish list ほしいものリスト	I am saving my money for: わたしがおかねをためているりゆう	
	My wish list / ほしいものリスト	**Price / きんがく**
1 一		
2 二		
3 三		

Money Log
マネーログ

My wallet
わたしのさいふのなか

Starting balance
はじめのおかね _____

Date 月／日	Description ないよう	Money received はいったおかね	Money spent つかったおかね	Balance のこったおかね

How much I saved so far / いままでで、たまったおかね _____

My piggy bank savings
わたしのちょきんばこのなか

Starting balance:
はじめのおかね _____

Date 月／日	Description ないよう	Money received はいったおかね	Money spent つかったおかね	Balance のこったおかね

How much I saved so far / いままでで、たまったおかね _____

Week of / こんしゅうのひづけ _____

Goals for this week こんしゅうのもくひょう	☆ Chores to complete 　　おてつだいをするかいすう _____	times かい
	☆ Money to earn: 　　こんしゅう、うけとりたいおかね _____	

Chores おてつだいのないよう	S にち	M げつ	T か	W すい	T もく	F きん	S ど
1 一 _____	○	○	○	○	○	○	○
2 二 _____	○	○	○	○	○	○	○
3 三 _____	○	○	○	○	○	○	○
4 四 _____	○	○	○	○	○	○	○
5 五 _____	○	○	○	○	○	○	○

Memo
メモ

☆ Results / けっか

This week, I completed chores   times
こんしゅう、おてつだいができたかいすう _____ かい

From my chores, I earned
おてつだいをして、うけとったおかね _____

From extra work, I earned extra
ついかのおてつだいをして、うけとったおかね _____

☆ Celebrate WINS! / せいかのおいわいをしましょう!

I am proud of myself for
できて、ほこりにおもうこと _____

I went above and beyond by doing
いつもより、もっとがんばってやりとげたこと _____

My wish list ほしいものリスト	I am saving my money for: わたしがおかねをためているりゆう	
	My wish list / ほしいものリスト	Price / きんがく
1 一		
2 二		
3 三		

Money Log
マネーログ

My wallet わたしのさいふのなか		Starting balance はじめのおかね _____		
Date 月／日	Description ないよう	Money received はいったおかね	Money spent つかったおかね	Balance のこったおかね

How much I saved so far / いままでで、たまったおかね _____

My piggy bank savings わたしのちょきんばこのなか		Starting balance: はじめのおかね _____		
Date 月／日	Description ないよう	Money received はいったおかね	Money spent つかったおかね	Balance のこったおかね

How much I saved so far / いままでで、たまったおかね _____

Week of / こんしゅうのひづけ _____

Goals for this week こんしゅうのもくひょう	☆ Chores to complete おてつだいをするかいすう _____	times かい
	☆ Money to earn: こんしゅう、うけとりたいおかね _____	

Chores おてつだいのないよう	S にち	M げつ	T か	W すい	T もく	F きん	S ど
1 一 _____	◯	◯	◯	◯	◯	◯	◯
2 二 _____	◯	◯	◯	◯	◯	◯	◯
3 三 _____	◯	◯	◯	◯	◯	◯	◯
4 四 _____	◯	◯	◯	◯	◯	◯	◯
5 五 _____	◯	◯	◯	◯	◯	◯	◯

Memo
メモ

☆ Results / けっか

This week, I completed chores
こんしゅう、おてつだいができたかいすう _____ times かい

From my chores, I earned
おてつだいをして、うけとったおかね _____

From extra work, I earned extra
ついかのおてつだいをして、うけとったおかね _____

☆ Celebrate WINS! / せいかのおいわいをしましょう!

I am proud of myself for
できて、ほこりにおもうこと _____

I went above and beyond by doing
いつもより、もっとがんばってやりとげたこと _____

My wish list ほしいものリスト	I am saving my money for: わたしがおかねをためているりゆう	
	My wish list / ほしいものリスト	Price / きんがく
1 一		
2 二		
3 三		

Money Log
マネーログ

My wallet わたしのさいふのなか		Starting balance はじめのおかね ＿＿＿＿＿＿＿		
Date 月／日	Description ないよう	Money received はいったおかね	Money spent つかったおかね	Balance のこったおかね

How much I saved so far / いままでで、たまったおかね ＿＿＿＿＿＿＿

My piggy bank savings わたしのちょきんばこのなか		Starting balance: はじめのおかね ＿＿＿＿＿＿		
Date 月／日	Description ないよう	Money received はいったおかね	Money spent つかったおかね	Balance のこったおかね

How much I saved so far / いままでで、たまったおかね ＿＿＿＿＿＿＿

Week of / こんしゅうのひづけ _____

Goals for this week こんしゅうのもくひょう	☆ Chores to complete おてつだいをするかいすう _____	times かい
	☆ Money to earn: こんしゅう、うけとりたいおかね _____	

Chores おてつだいのないよう	S にち	M げつ	T か	W すい	T もく	F きん	S ど
1 一 _____	○	○	○	○	○	○	○
2 二 _____	○	○	○	○	○	○	○
3 三 _____	○	○	○	○	○	○	○
4 四 _____	○	○	○	○	○	○	○
5 五 _____	○	○	○	○	○	○	○

Memo メモ

☆ Results / けっか

This week, I completed chores   times
こんしゅう、おてつだいができたかいすう _____ かい

From my chores, I earned
おてつだいをして、うけとったおかね _____

From extra work, I earned extra
ついかのおてつだいをして、うけとったおかね _____

☆ Celebrate WINS! / せいかのおいわいをしましょう!

I am proud of myself for
できて、ほこりにおもうこと _____

I went above and beyond by doing
いつもより、もっとがんばってやりとげたこと _____

My wish list ほしいものリスト	I am saving my money for: わたしがおかねをためているりゆう	
	My wish list / ほしいものリスト	Price / きんがく
1 一		
2 二		
3 三		

Money Log
マネーログ

My wallet わたしのさいふのなか		Starting balance はじめのおかね ＿＿＿＿＿＿		
Date 月／日	Description ないよう	Money received はいったおかね	Money spent つかったおかね	Balance のこったおかね

How much I saved so far / いままでで、たまったおかね ＿＿＿＿＿＿

My piggy bank savings わたしのちょきんばこのなか		Starting balance: はじめのおかね ＿＿＿＿＿		
Date 月／日	Description ないよう	Money received はいったおかね	Money spent つかったおかね	Balance のこったおかね

How much I saved so far / いままでで、たまったおかね ＿＿＿＿＿＿

Week of / こんしゅうのひづけ _____

Goals for this week
こんしゅうのもくひょう

☆ Chores to complete   times
   おてつだいをするかいすう _____ かい
☆ Money to earn:
   こんしゅう、うけとりたいおかね _____

Chores おてつだいのないよう	S にち	M げつ	T か	W すい	T もく	F きん	S ど
1 一 _____	○	○	○	○	○	○	○
2 二 _____	○	○	○	○	○	○	○
3 三 _____	○	○	○	○	○	○	○
4 四 _____	○	○	○	○	○	○	○
5 五 _____	○	○	○	○	○	○	○

Memo
メモ

☆ Results / けっか

This week, I completed chores   times
こんしゅう、おてつだいができたかいすう _____ かい

From my chores, I earned
おてつだいをして、うけとったおかね _____

From extra work, I earned extra
ついかのおてつだいをして、うけとったおかね _____

☆ Celebrate WINS! / せいかのおいわいをしましょう!

I am proud of myself for
できて、ほこりにおもうこと _____

I went above and beyond by doing
いつもより、もっとがんばってやりとげたこと _____

My wish list ほしいものリスト	I am saving my money for: わたしがおかねをためているりゆう	
	My wish list / ほしいものリスト	Price / きんがく
1 一		
2 二		
3 三		

Money Log
マネーログ

My wallet わたしのさいふのなか		Starting balance はじめのおかね _____		
Date 月／日	Description ないよう	Money received はいったおかね	Money spent つかったおかね	Balance のこったおかね

How much I saved so far / いままでで、たまったおかね _____

My piggy bank savings わたしのちょきんばこのなか		Starting balance: はじめのおかね _____		
Date 月／日	Description ないよう	Money received はいったおかね	Money spent つかったおかね	Balance のこったおかね

How much I saved so far / いままでで、たまったおかね _____

Week of / こんしゅうのひづけ _____

Goals for this week こんしゅうのもくひょう	☆ Chores to complete おてつだいをするかいすう _____	times かい
	☆ Money to earn: こんしゅう、うけとりたいおかね _____	

Chores おてつだいのないよう	S にち	M げつ	T か	W すい	T もく	F きん	S ど
1 一 _____	○	○	○	○	○	○	○
2 二 _____	○	○	○	○	○	○	○
3 三 _____	○	○	○	○	○	○	○
4 四 _____	○	○	○	○	○	○	○
5 五 _____	○	○	○	○	○	○	○

Memo
メモ

☆ Results / けっか

This week, I completed chores   times
こんしゅう、おてつだいができたかいすう _____ かい

From my chores, I earned
おてつだいをして、うけとったおかね _____

From extra work, I earned extra
ついかのおてつだいをして、うけとったおかね _____

☆ Celebrate WINS! / せいかのおいわいをしましょう!

I am proud of myself for
できて、ほこりにおもうこと _____

I went above and beyond by doing
いつもより、もっとがんばってやりとげたこと _____

My wish list ほしいものリスト	I am saving my money for: わたしがおかねをためているりゆう	
	My wish list / ほしいものリスト	Price / きんがく
1 一		
2 二		
3 三		

Money Log
マネーログ

My wallet
わたしのさいふのなか

Starting balance
はじめのおかね _____

Date 月／日	Description ないよう	Money received はいったおかね	Money spent つかったおかね	Balance のこったおかね

How much I saved so far / いままでで、たまったおかね _____

My piggy bank savings
わたしのちょきんばこのなか

Starting balance:
はじめのおかね _____

Date 月／日	Description ないよう	Money received はいったおかね	Money spent つかったおかね	Balance のこったおかね

How much I saved so far / いままでで、たまったおかね _____

Week of / こんしゅうのひづけ _____

| Goals for this week
こんしゅうのもくひょう | ☆ Chores to complete
おてつだいをするかいすう _____ | times
かい |
| | ☆ Money to earn:
こんしゅう、うけとりたいおかね _____ | |

Chores おてつだいのないよう	S にち	M げつ	T か	W すい	T もく	F きん	S ど
1 一 _____	○	○	○	○	○	○	○
2 二 _____	○	○	○	○	○	○	○
3 三 _____	○	○	○	○	○	○	○
4 四 _____	○	○	○	○	○	○	○
5 五 _____	○	○	○	○	○	○	○

Memo
メモ

☆ Results / けっか

This week, I completed chores   times
こんしゅう、おてつだいができたかいすう _____ かい

From my chores, I earned
おてつだいをして、うけとったおかね _____

From extra work, I earned extra
ついかのおてつだいをして、うけとったおかね _____

☆ Celebrate WINS! / せいかのおいわいをしましょう!

I am proud of myself for
できて、ほこりにおもうこと _____

I went above and beyond by doing
いつもより、もっとがんばってやりとげたこと _____

My wish list ほしいものリスト	I am saving my money for: わたしがおかねをためているりゆう	
	My wish list / ほしいものリスト	Price / きんがく
1 一		
2 二		
3 三		

Money Log
マネーログ

My wallet
わたしのさいふのなか

Starting balance
はじめのおかね _____

Date 月／日	Description ないよう	Money received はいったおかね	Money spent つかったおかね	Balance のこったおかね

How much I saved so far / いままでで、たまったおかね _____

My piggy bank savings
わたしのちょきんばこのなか

Starting balance:
はじめのおかね _____

Date 月／日	Description ないよう	Money received はいったおかね	Money spent つかったおかね	Balance のこったおかね

How much I saved so far / いままでで、たまったおかね _____

Week of / こんしゅうのひづけ _____

| Goals for this week
こんしゅうのもくひょう | ☆ Chores to complete
おてつだいをするかいすう _____
☆ Money to earn:
こんしゅう、うけとりたいおかね _____ | times
かい |

Chores おてつだいのないよう	S にち	M げつ	T か	W すい	T もく	F きん	S ど
1 一 _____	◯	◯	◯	◯	◯	◯	◯
2 二 _____	◯	◯	◯	◯	◯	◯	◯
3 三 _____	◯	◯	◯	◯	◯	◯	◯
4 四 _____	◯	◯	◯	◯	◯	◯	◯
5 五 _____	◯	◯	◯	◯	◯	◯	◯

Memo
メモ

☆ Results / けっか

This week, I completed chores   times
こんしゅう、おてつだいができたかいすう _____ かい

From my chores, I earned
おてつだいをして、うけとったおかね _____

From extra work, I earned extra
ついかのおてつだいをして、うけとったおかね _____

☆ Celebrate WINS! / せいかのおいわいをしましょう!

I am proud of myself for
できて、ほこりにおもうこと _____

I went above and beyond by doing
いつもより、もっとがんばってやりとげたこと _____

My wish list ほしいものリスト	I am saving my money for: わたしがおかねをためているりゆう	
	My wish list / ほしいものリスト	**Price / きんがく**
1 一		
2 二		
3 三		

Money Log
マネーログ

My wallet
わたしのさいふのなか　　　　　　　　　　Starting balance
はじめのおかね _____

Date 月／日	Description ないよう	Money received はいったおかね	Money spent つかったおかね	Balance のこったおかね

How much I saved so far / いままでで、たまったおかね _____

My piggy bank savings
わたしのちょきんばこのなか　　　　　　Starting balance:
はじめのおかね _____

Date 月／日	Description ないよう	Money received はいったおかね	Money spent つかったおかね	Balance のこったおかね

How much I saved so far / いままでで、たまったおかね _____

Week of / こんしゅうのひづけ _____

| Goals for this week
こんしゅうのもくひょう | ☆ Chores to complete times
おてつだいをするかいすう _____ かい
☆ Money to earn:
こんしゅう、うけとりたいおかね _____ |

Chores おてつだいのないよう	S にち	M げつ	T か	W すい	T もく	F きん	S ど
1 一 _____	○	○	○	○	○	○	○
2 二 _____	○	○	○	○	○	○	○
3 三 _____	○	○	○	○	○	○	○
4 四 _____	○	○	○	○	○	○	○
5 五 _____	○	○	○	○	○	○	○

| Memo
メモ |

☆ Results / けっか

This week, I completed chores times
こんしゅう、おてつだいができたかいすう _____ かい

From my chores, I earned
おてつだいをして、うけとったおかね _____

From extra work, I earned extra
ついかのおてつだいをして、うけとったおかね _____

☆ Celebrate WINS! / せいかのおいわいをしましょう!

I am proud of myself for
できて、ほこりにおもうこと _____

I went above and beyond by doing
いつもより、もっとがんばってやりとげたこと _____

My wish list ほしいものリスト	I am saving my money for: わたしがおかねをためているりゆう	
	My wish list / ほしいものリスト	Price / きんがく
1 一		
2 二		
3 三		

Money Log
マネーログ

My wallet わたしのさいふのなか		Starting balance はじめのおかね _____		
Date 月／日	Description ないよう	Money received はいったおかね	Money spent つかったおかね	Balance のこったおかね

How much I saved so far / いままでで、たまったおかね _____

My piggy bank savings わたしのちょきんばこのなか		Starting balance: はじめのおかね _____		
Date 月／日	Description ないよう	Money received はいったおかね	Money spent つかったおかね	Balance のこったおかね

How much I saved so far / いままでで、たまったおかね _____

Week of / こんしゅうのひづけ _____

Goals for this week こんしゅうのもくひょう	☆ Chores to complete おてつだいをするかいすう _____	times かい
	☆ Money to earn: こんしゅう、うけとりたいおかね _____	

Chores おてつだいのないよう	S にち	M げつ	T か	W すい	T もく	F きん	S ど
1 一 _____	○	○	○	○	○	○	○
2 二 _____	○	○	○	○	○	○	○
3 三 _____	○	○	○	○	○	○	○
4 四 _____	○	○	○	○	○	○	○
5 五 _____	○	○	○	○	○	○	○

Memo
メモ

☆ Results / けっか

This week, I completed chores   times
こんしゅう、おてつだいができたかいすう _____ かい

From my chores, I earned
おてつだいをして、うけとったおかね _____

From extra work, I earned extra
ついかのおてつだいをして、うけとったおかね _____

☆ Celebrate WINS! / せいかのおいわいをしましょう!

I am proud of myself for
できて、ほこりにおもうこと _____

I went above and beyond by doing
いつもより、もっとがんばってやりとげたこと _____

My wish list
ほしいものリスト

I am saving my money for:
わたしがおかねをためているりゆう

	My wish list / ほしいものリスト	Price / きんがく
1 一		
2 二		
3 三		

 # Money Log
マネーログ

My wallet
わたしのさいふのなか

Starting balance
はじめのおかね _____

Date 月／日	Description ないよう	Money received はいったおかね	Money spent つかったおかね	Balance のこったおかね

How much I saved so far / いままでで、たまったおかね _____

My piggy bank savings
わたしのちょきんばこのなか

Starting balance:
はじめのおかね _____

Date 月／日	Description ないよう	Money received はいったおかね	Money spent つかったおかね	Balance のこったおかね

How much I saved so far / いままでで、たまったおかね _____

Week of / こんしゅうのひづけ _____

Goals for this week こんしゅうのもくひょう	☆ Chores to complete 　おてつだいをするかいすう _____	times かい
	☆ Money to earn: 　こんしゅう、うけとりたいおかね _____	

Chores おてつだいのないよう	S にち	M げつ	T か	W すい	T もく	F きん	S ど
1 一 _____	○	○	○	○	○	○	○
2 二 _____	○	○	○	○	○	○	○
3 三 _____	○	○	○	○	○	○	○
4 四 _____	○	○	○	○	○	○	○
5 五 _____	○	○	○	○	○	○	○

Memo
メモ

☆ Results / けっか

This week, I completed chores   times
こんしゅう、おてつだいができたかいすう _____ かい

From my chores, I earned
おてつだいをして、うけとったおかね _____

From extra work, I earned extra
ついかのおてつだいをして、うけとったおかね _____

☆ Celebrate WINS! / せいかのおいわいをしましょう!

I am proud of myself for
できて、ほこりにおもうこと _____

I went above and beyond by doing
いつもより、もっとがんばってやりとげたこと _____

My wish list ほしいものリスト	I am saving my money for: わたしがおかねをためているりゆう	
	My wish list / ほしいものリスト	Price / きんがく
1 一		
2 二		
3 三		

Money Log
マネーログ

My wallet わたしのさいふのなか		Starting balance はじめのおかね _____		
Date 月／日	Description ないよう	Money received はいったおかね	Money spent つかったおかね	Balance のこったおかね

How much I saved so far / いままでで、たまったおかね _____

My piggy bank savings わたしのちょきんばこのなか		Starting balance: はじめのおかね _____		
Date 月／日	Description ないよう	Money received はいったおかね	Money spent つかったおかね	Balance のこったおかね

How much I saved so far / いままでで、たまったおかね _____

Week of / こんしゅうのひづけ _____

Goals for this week
こんしゅうのもくひょう

☆ Chores to complete   times
おてつだいをするかいすう _____ かい

☆ Money to earn:
こんしゅう、うけとりたいおかね _____

Chores おてつだいのないよう	S にち	M げつ	T か	W すい	T もく	F きん	S ど
1 一 _____	○	○	○	○	○	○	○
2 二 _____	○	○	○	○	○	○	○
3 三 _____	○	○	○	○	○	○	○
4 四 _____	○	○	○	○	○	○	○
5 五 _____	○	○	○	○	○	○	○

Memo
メモ

☆ Results / けっか

This week, I completed chores   times
こんしゅう、おてつだいができたかいすう _____ かい

From my chores, I earned
おてつだいをして、うけとったおかね _____

From extra work, I earned extra
ついかのおてつだいをして、うけとったおかね _____

☆ Celebrate WINS! / せいかのおいわいをしましょう!

I am proud of myself for
できて、ほこりにおもうこと _____

I went above and beyond by doing
いつもより、もっとがんばってやりとげたこと _____

My wish list ほしいものリスト	I am saving my money for: わたしがおかねをためているりゆう	
	My wish list / ほしいものリスト	Price / きんがく
1 一		
2 二		
3 三		

Money Log
マネーログ

My wallet
わたしのさいふのなか   Starting balance
                              はじめのおかね _____

Date 月／日	Description ないよう	Money received はいったおかね	Money spent つかったおかね	Balance のこったおかね

How much I saved so far / いままでで、たまったおかね _____

My piggy bank savings
わたしのちょきんばこのなか   Starting balance:
                                   はじめのおかね _____

Date 月／日	Description ないよう	Money received はいったおかね	Money spent つかったおかね	Balance のこったおかね

How much I saved so far / いままでで、たまったおかね _____

Week of / こんしゅうのひづけ _____

Goals for this week
こんしゅうのもくひょう

☆ Chores to complete
おてつだいをするかいすう _____ times かい

☆ Money to earn:
こんしゅう、うけとりたいおかね _____

Chores おてつだいのないよう	S にち	M げつ	T か	W すい	T もく	F きん	S ど
1 一 _____	○	○	○	○	○	○	○
2 二 _____	○	○	○	○	○	○	○
3 三 _____	○	○	○	○	○	○	○
4 四 _____	○	○	○	○	○	○	○
5 五 _____	○	○	○	○	○	○	○

Memo
メモ

☆ Results / けっか

This week, I completed chores
こんしゅう、おてつだいができたかいすう _____ times かい

From my chores, I earned
おてつだいをして、うけとったおかね _____

From extra work, I earned extra
ついかのおてつだいをして、うけとったおかね _____

☆ Celebrate WINS! / せいかのおいわいをしましょう!

I am proud of myself for
できて、ほこりにおもうこと _____

I went above and beyond by doing
いつもより、もっとがんばってやりとげたこと _____

My wish list ほしいものリスト	I am saving my money for: わたしがおかねをためているりゆう	
	My wish list / ほしいものリスト	Price / きんがく
1 　一		
2 　二		
3 　三		

Money Log
マネーログ

My wallet
わたしのさいふのなか　　　　　　Starting balance
　　　　　　　　　　　　　　　　はじめのおかね _____

Date 月／日	Description ないよう	Money received はいったおかね	Money spent つかったおかね	Balance のこったおかね

How much I saved so far / いままでで、たまったおかね _____

My piggy bank savings
わたしのちょきんばこのなか　　　Starting balance:
　　　　　　　　　　　　　　　　はじめのおかね _____

Date 月／日	Description ないよう	Money received はいったおかね	Money spent つかったおかね	Balance のこったおかね

How much I saved so far / いままでで、たまったおかね _____

Week of / こんしゅうのひづけ _____

Goals for this week
こんしゅうのもくひょう

☆ **Chores to complete**   times
   おてつだいをするかいすう _____ かい
☆ **Money to earn:**
   こんしゅう、うけとりたいおかね _____

Chores おてつだいのないよう	S にち	M げつ	T か	W すい	T もく	F きん	S ど
1 一 _____	◯	◯	◯	◯	◯	◯	◯
2 二 _____	◯	◯	◯	◯	◯	◯	◯
3 三 _____	◯	◯	◯	◯	◯	◯	◯
4 四 _____	◯	◯	◯	◯	◯	◯	◯
5 五 _____	◯	◯	◯	◯	◯	◯	◯

Memo
メモ

☆ Results / けっか

This week, I completed chores   times
こんしゅう、おてつだいができたかいすう _____ かい

From my chores, I earned
おてつだいをして、うけとったおかね _____

From extra work, I earned extra
ついかのおてつだいをして、うけとったおかね _____

☆ Celebrate WINS! / せいかのおいわいをしましょう!

I am proud of myself for
できて、ほこりにおもうこと _____

I went above and beyond by doing
いつもより、もっとがんばってやりとげたこと _____

My wish list ほしいものリスト	I am saving my money for: わたしがおかねをためているりゆう	
	My wish list / ほしいものリスト	Price / きんがく
1 一		
2 二		
3 三		

Money Log
マネーログ

My wallet わたしのさいふのなか		Starting balance はじめのおかね _____		
Date 月／日	Description ないよう	Money received はいったおかね	Money spent つかったおかね	Balance のこったおかね

How much I saved so far / いままでで、たまったおかね _____

My piggy bank savings わたしのちょきんばこのなか		Starting balance: はじめのおかね _____		
Date 月／日	Description ないよう	Money received はいったおかね	Money spent つかったおかね	Balance のこったおかね

How much I saved so far / いままでで、たまったおかね _____

Week of / こんしゅうのひづけ _____

Goals for this week こんしゅうのもくひょう	☆ Chores to complete おてつだいをするかいすう _____	times かい
	☆ Money to earn: こんしゅう、うけとりたいおかね _____	

Chores おてつだいのないよう	S にち	M げつ	T か	W すい	T もく	F きん	S ど
1 一 _____	◯	◯	◯	◯	◯	◯	◯
2 二 _____	◯	◯	◯	◯	◯	◯	◯
3 三 _____	◯	◯	◯	◯	◯	◯	◯
4 四 _____	◯	◯	◯	◯	◯	◯	◯
5 五 _____	◯	◯	◯	◯	◯	◯	◯

Memo
メモ

☆ Results / けっか

This week, I completed chores   times
こんしゅう、おてつだいができたかいすう _____ かい

From my chores, I earned
おてつだいをして、うけとったおかね _____

From extra work, I earned extra
ついかのおてつだいをして、うけとったおかね _____

☆ Celebrate WINS! / せいかのおいわいをしましょう!

I am proud of myself for
できて、ほこりにおもうこと _____

I went above and beyond by doing
いつもより、もっとがんばってやりとげたこと _____

My wish list ほしいものリスト	I am saving my money for: わたしがおかねをためているりゆう	
	My wish list / ほしいものリスト	Price / きんがく
1 一		
2 二		
3 三		

Money Log
マネーログ

My wallet
わたしのさいふのなか

Starting balance
はじめのおかね _____

Date 月／日	Description ないよう	Money received はいったおかね	Money spent つかったおかね	Balance のこったおかね

How much I saved so far / いままでで、たまったおかね _____

My piggy bank savings
わたしのちょきんばこのなか

Starting balance:
はじめのおかね _____

Date 月／日	Description ないよう	Money received はいったおかね	Money spent つかったおかね	Balance のこったおかね

How much I saved so far / いままでで、たまったおかね _____

Week of / こんしゅうのひづけ _____

Goals for this week こんしゅうのもくひょう	☆ Chores to complete おてつだいをするかいすう _____	times かい
	☆ Money to earn: こんしゅう、うけとりたいおかね _____	

Chores おてつだいのないよう	S にち	M げつ	T か	W すい	T もく	F きん	S ど
1 一 _____	○	○	○	○	○	○	○
2 二 _____	○	○	○	○	○	○	○
3 三 _____	○	○	○	○	○	○	○
4 四 _____	○	○	○	○	○	○	○
5 五 _____	○	○	○	○	○	○	○

Memo
メモ

☆ Results / けっか

This week, I completed chores   times
こんしゅう、おてつだいができたかいすう _____ かい

From my chores, I earned
おてつだいをして、うけとったおかね _____

From extra work, I earned extra
ついかのおてつだいをして、うけとったおかね _____

☆ Celebrate WINS! / せいかのおいわいをしましょう!

I am proud of myself for
できて、ほこりにおもうこと _____

I went above and beyond by doing
いつもより、もっとがんばってやりとげたこと _____

My wish list
ほしいものリスト

I am saving my money for:
わたしがおかねをためているりゆう

	My wish list / ほしいものリスト	Price / きんがく
1 —		
2 二		
3 三		

 # Money Log
マネーログ

My wallet
わたしのさいふのなか

Starting balance
はじめのおかね _____

Date 月／日	Description ないよう	Money received はいったおかね	Money spent つかったおかね	Balance のこったおかね

How much I saved so far / いままでで、たまったおかね _____

My piggy bank savings
わたしのちょきんばこのなか

Starting balance:
はじめのおかね _____

Date 月／日	Description ないよう	Money received はいったおかね	Money spent つかったおかね	Balance のこったおかね

How much I saved so far / いままでで、たまったおかね _____

Week of / こんしゅうのひづけ _____

Goals for this week こんしゅうのもくひょう	☆ Chores to complete おてつだいをするかいすう _____	times かい
	☆ Money to earn: こんしゅう、うけとりたいおかね _____	

Chores おてつだいのないよう	S にち	M げつ	T か	W すい	T もく	F きん	S ど
1 一 _____	○	○	○	○	○	○	○
2 二 _____	○	○	○	○	○	○	○
3 三 _____	○	○	○	○	○	○	○
4 四 _____	○	○	○	○	○	○	○
5 五 _____	○	○	○	○	○	○	○

Memo
メモ

☆ Results / けっか

This week, I completed chores _____ times
こんしゅう、おてつだいができたかいすう _____ かい

From my chores, I earned
おてつだいをして、うけとったおかね _____

From extra work, I earned extra
ついかのおてつだいをして、うけとったおかね _____

☆ Celebrate WINS! / せいかのおいわいをしましょう!

I am proud of myself for
できて、ほこりにおもうこと _____

I went above and beyond by doing
いつもより、もっとがんばってやりとげたこと _____

My wish list ほしいものリスト	I am saving my money for: わたしがおかねをためているりゆう	
	My wish list / ほしいものリスト	**Price / きんがく**
1 一		
2 二		
3 三		

 # Money Log
マネーログ

My wallet わたしのさいふのなか		Starting balance はじめのおかね _____		
Date 月／日	**Description ないよう**	**Money received はいったおかね**	**Money spent つかったおかね**	**Balance のこったおかね**

How much I saved so far / いままでで、たまったおかね _____

My piggy bank savings わたしのちょきんばこのなか		Starting balance: はじめのおかね _____		
Date 月／日	**Description ないよう**	**Money received はいったおかね**	**Money spent つかったおかね**	**Balance のこったおかね**

How much I saved so far / いままでで、たまったおかね _____

Week of / こんしゅうのひづけ _____

| Goals for this week
こんしゅうのもくひょう | ☆ Chores to complete   times
   おてつだいをするかいすう _____ かい
☆ Money to earn:
   こんしゅう、うけとりたいおかね _____ |

Chores おてつだいのないよう	S にち	M げつ	T か	W すい	T もく	F きん	S ど
1 一 _____	○	○	○	○	○	○	○
2 二 _____	○	○	○	○	○	○	○
3 三 _____	○	○	○	○	○	○	○
4 四 _____	○	○	○	○	○	○	○
5 五 _____	○	○	○	○	○	○	○

| Memo
メモ |

☆ Results / けっか

This week, I completed chores   times
こんしゅう、おてつだいができたかいすう _____ かい

From my chores, I earned
おてつだいをして、うけとったおかね _____

From extra work, I earned extra
ついかのおてつだいをして、うけとったおかね _____

☆ Celebrate WINS! / せいかのおいわいをしましょう!

I am proud of myself for
できて、ほこりにおもうこと _____

I went above and beyond by doing
いつもより、もっとがんばってやりとげたこと _____

54

My wish list ほしいものリスト	I am saving my money for: わたしがおかねをためているりゆう	

	My wish list / ほしいものリスト	Price / きんがく
1 一		
2 二		
3 三		

Money Log
マネーログ

My wallet
わたしのさいふのなか   **Starting balance**
はじめのおかね _____

Date 月／日	Description ないよう	Money received はいったおかね	Money spent つかったおかね	Balance のこったおかね

How much I saved so far / いままでで、たまったおかね _____

My piggy bank savings
わたしのちょきんばこのなか   **Starting balance:**
はじめのおかね _____

Date 月／日	Description ないよう	Money received はいったおかね	Money spent つかったおかね	Balance のこったおかね

How much I saved so far / いままでで、たまったおかね _____

Week of / こんしゅうのひづけ _____

Goals for this week こんしゅうのもくひょう	☆ Chores to complete おてつだいをするかいすう _____	times かい
	☆ Money to earn: こんしゅう、うけとりたいおかね _____	

Chores おてつだいのないよう	S にち	M げつ	T か	W すい	T もく	F きん	S ど
1 一 _____	○	○	○	○	○	○	○
2 二 _____	○	○	○	○	○	○	○
3 三 _____	○	○	○	○	○	○	○
4 四 _____	○	○	○	○	○	○	○
5 五 _____	○	○	○	○	○	○	○

Memo
メモ

☆ Results / けっか

This week, I completed chores   times
こんしゅう、おてつだいができたかいすう _____ かい

From my chores, I earned
おてつだいをして、うけとったおかね _____

From extra work, I earned extra
ついかのおてつだいをして、うけとったおかね _____

☆ Celebrate WINS! / せいかのおいわいをしましょう!

I am proud of myself for
できて、ほこりにおもうこと _____

I went above and beyond by doing
いつもより、もっとがんばってやりとげたこと _____

My wish list ほしいものリスト	I am saving my money for: わたしがおかねをためているりゆう		
	My wish list / ほしいものリスト		Price / きんがく
1 一			
2 二			
3 三			

 # Money Log
マネーログ

My wallet わたしのさいふのなか		Starting balance はじめのおかね _____		
Date 月／日	Description ないよう	Money received はいったおかね	Money spent つかったおかね	Balance のこったおかね

How much I saved so far / いままでで、たまったおかね _____

My piggy bank savings わたしのちょきんばこのなか		Starting balance: はじめのおかね _____		
Date 月／日	Description ないよう	Money received はいったおかね	Money spent つかったおかね	Balance のこったおかね

How much I saved so far / いままでで、たまったおかね _____

Week of / こんしゅうのひづけ _____

Goals for this week こんしゅうのもくひょう	☆ Chores to complete おてつだいをするかいすう _____	times かい
	☆ Money to earn: こんしゅう、うけとりたいおかね _____	

Chores おてつだいのないよう	S にち	M げつ	T か	W すい	T もく	F きん	S ど
1 一 _____	○	○	○	○	○	○	○
2 二 _____	○	○	○	○	○	○	○
3 三 _____	○	○	○	○	○	○	○
4 四 _____	○	○	○	○	○	○	○
5 五 _____	○	○	○	○	○	○	○

Memo メモ

☆ Results / けっか

This week, I completed chores   times
こんしゅう、おてつだいができたかいすう _____ かい

From my chores, I earned
おてつだいをして、うけとったおかね _____

From extra work, I earned extra
ついかのおてつだいをして、うけとったおかね _____

☆ Celebrate WINS! / せいかのおいわいをしましょう!

I am proud of myself for
できて、ほこりにおもうこと _____

I went above and beyond by doing
いつもより、もっとがんばってやりとげたこと _____

My wish list ほしいものリスト	I am saving my money for: わたしがおかねをためているりゆう	
	My wish list / ほしいものリスト	Price / きんがく
1 一		
2 二		
3 三		

Money Log
マネーログ

My wallet
わたしのさいふのなか

Starting balance
はじめのおかね _____

Date 月／日	Description ないよう	Money received はいったおかね	Money spent つかったおかね	Balance のこったおかね

How much I saved so far / いままでで、たまったおかね _____

My piggy bank savings
わたしのちょきんばこのなか

Starting balance:
はじめのおかね _____

Date 月／日	Description ないよう	Money received はいったおかね	Money spent つかったおかね	Balance のこったおかね

How much I saved so far / いままでで、たまったおかね _____

Week of / こんしゅうのひづけ _____

Goals for this week こんしゅうのもくひょう	☆ Chores to complete おてつだいをするかいすう _____	times かい
	☆ Money to earn: こんしゅう、うけとりたいおかね _____	

Chores おてつだいのないよう	S にち	M げつ	T か	W すい	T もく	F きん	S ど
1 一 _____	○	○	○	○	○	○	○
2 二 _____	○	○	○	○	○	○	○
3 三 _____	○	○	○	○	○	○	○
4 四 _____	○	○	○	○	○	○	○
5 五 _____	○	○	○	○	○	○	○

Memo
メモ

☆ Results / けっか

This week, I completed chores
こんしゅう、おてつだいができたかいすう _____ times かい

From my chores, I earned
おてつだいをして、うけとったおかね _____

From extra work, I earned extra
ついかのおてつだいをして、うけとったおかね _____

☆ Celebrate WINS! / せいかのおいわいをしましょう!

I am proud of myself for
できて、ほこりにおもうこと _____

I went above and beyond by doing
いつもより、もっとがんばってやりとげたこと _____

My wish list ほしいものリスト	I am saving my money for: わたしがおかねをためているりゆう	
	My wish list / ほしいものリスト	Price / きんがく
1 一		
2 二		
3 三		

Money Log
マネーログ

My wallet
わたしのさいふのなか   Starting balance
                              はじめのおかね _____

Date 月／日	Description ないよう	Money received はいったおかね	Money spent つかったおかね	Balance のこったおかね

How much I saved so far / いままでで、たまったおかね _____

My piggy bank savings
わたしのちょきんばこのなか   Starting balance:
                                 はじめのおかね _____

Date 月／日	Description ないよう	Money received はいったおかね	Money spent つかったおかね	Balance のこったおかね

How much I saved so far / いままでで、たまったおかね _____

Week of / こんしゅうのひづけ _____

Goals for this week こんしゅうのもくひょう	☆ Chores to complete おてつだいをするかいすう _____	times かい
	☆ Money to earn: こんしゅう、うけとりたいおかね _____	

Chores おてつだいのないよう	S にち	M げつ	T か	W すい	T もく	F きん	S ど
1 一 _____	○	○	○	○	○	○	○
2 二 _____	○	○	○	○	○	○	○
3 三 _____	○	○	○	○	○	○	○
4 四 _____	○	○	○	○	○	○	○
5 五 _____	○	○	○	○	○	○	○

Memo
メモ

☆ Results / けっか

This week, I completed chores   times
こんしゅう、おてつだいができたかいすう _____ かい

From my chores, I earned
おてつだいをして、うけとったおかね _____

From extra work, I earned extra
ついかのおてつだいをして、うけとったおかね _____

☆ Celebrate WINS! / せいかのおいわいをしましょう!

I am proud of myself for
できて、ほこりにおもうこと _____

I went above and beyond by doing
いつもより、もっとがんばってやりとげたこと _____

My wish list ほしいものリスト	I am saving my money for: わたしがおかねをためているりゆう	
	My wish list / ほしいものリスト	Price / きんがく
1 一		
2 二		
3 三		

Money Log
マネーログ

My wallet
わたしのさいふのなか

Starting balance
はじめのおかね _____

Date 月／日	Description ないよう	Money received はいったおかね	Money spent つかったおかね	Balance のこったおかね

How much I saved so far / いままでで、たまったおかね _____

My piggy bank savings
わたしのちょきんばこのなか

Starting balance:
はじめのおかね _____

Date 月／日	Description ないよう	Money received はいったおかね	Money spent つかったおかね	Balance のこったおかね

How much I saved so far / いままでで、たまったおかね _____

Week of / こんしゅうのひづけ _____

Goals for this week こんしゅうのもくひょう	☆ Chores to complete おてつだいをするかいすう _____	times かい
	☆ Money to earn: こんしゅう、うけとりたいおかね _____	

Chores おてつだいのないよう	S にち	M げつ	T か	W すい	T もく	F きん	S ど
1 一 _____	○	○	○	○	○	○	○
2 二 _____	○	○	○	○	○	○	○
3 三 _____	○	○	○	○	○	○	○
4 四 _____	○	○	○	○	○	○	○
5 五 _____	○	○	○	○	○	○	○

Memo
メモ

☆ Results / けっか

This week, I completed chores   times
こんしゅう、おてつだいができたかいすう _____ かい

From my chores, I earned
おてつだいをして、うけとったおかね _____

From extra work, I earned extra
ついかのおてつだいをして、うけとったおかね _____

☆ Celebrate WINS! / せいかのおいわいをしましょう!

I am proud of myself for
できて、ほこりにおもうこと _____

I went above and beyond by doing
いつもより、もっとがんばってやりとげたこと _____

My wish list ほしいものリスト	I am saving my money for: わたしがおかねをためているりゆう	
	My wish list / ほしいものリスト	Price / きんがく
1 一		
2 二		
3 三		

Money Log
マネーログ

My wallet わたしのさいふのなか		Starting balance はじめのおかね _____		
Date 月／日	Description ないよう	Money received はいったおかね	Money spent つかったおかね	Balance のこったおかね

How much I saved so far / いままでで、たまったおかね _____

My piggy bank savings わたしのちょきんばこのなか		Starting balance: はじめのおかね _____		
Date 月／日	Description ないよう	Money received はいったおかね	Money spent つかったおかね	Balance のこったおかね

How much I saved so far / いままでで、たまったおかね _____

Week of / こんしゅうのひづけ _____

Goals for this week
こんしゅうのもくひょう

☆ Chores to complete
おてつだいをするかいすう _____ times かい

☆ Money to earn:
こんしゅう、うけとりたいおかね _____

Chores おてつだいのないよう	S にち	M げつ	T か	W すい	T もく	F きん	S ど
1 一 _____	○	○	○	○	○	○	○
2 二 _____	○	○	○	○	○	○	○
3 三 _____	○	○	○	○	○	○	○
4 四 _____	○	○	○	○	○	○	○
5 五 _____	○	○	○	○	○	○	○

Memo
メモ

☆ Results / けっか

This week, I completed chores
こんしゅう、おてつだいができたかいすう _____ times かい

From my chores, I earned
おてつだいをして、うけとったおかね _____

From extra work, I earned extra
ついかのおてつだいをして、うけとったおかね _____

☆ Celebrate WINS! / せいかのおいわいをしましょう!

I am proud of myself for
できて、ほこりにおもうこと _____

I went above and beyond by doing
いつもより、もっとがんばってやりとげたこと _____

My wish list ほしいものリスト	I am saving my money for: わたしがおかねをためているりゆう	
	My wish list / ほしいものリスト	Price / きんがく
1 一		
2 二		
3 三		

 # Money Log
マネーログ

My wallet
わたしのさいふのなか

Starting balance
はじめのおかね _____

Date 月／日	Description ないよう	Money received はいったおかね	Money spent つかったおかね	Balance のこったおかね

How much I saved so far / いままでで、たまったおかね _____

My piggy bank savings
わたしのちょきんばこのなか

Starting balance:
はじめのおかね _____

Date 月／日	Description ないよう	Money received はいったおかね	Money spent つかったおかね	Balance のこったおかね

How much I saved so far / いままでで、たまったおかね _____

Week of / こんしゅうのひづけ _____

Goals for this week こんしゅうのもくひょう	☆ Chores to complete おてつだいをするかいすう _____	times かい
	☆ Money to earn: こんしゅう、うけとりたいおかね _____	

Chores おてつだいのないよう	S にち	M げつ	T か	W すい	T もく	F きん	S ど
1 一 _____	◯	◯	◯	◯	◯	◯	◯
2 二 _____	◯	◯	◯	◯	◯	◯	◯
3 三 _____	◯	◯	◯	◯	◯	◯	◯
4 四 _____	◯	◯	◯	◯	◯	◯	◯
5 五 _____	◯	◯	◯	◯	◯	◯	◯

Memo
メモ

☆ Results / けっか

This week, I completed chores
こんしゅう、おてつだいができたかいすう _____ times かい

From my chores, I earned
おてつだいをして、うけとったおかね _____

From extra work, I earned extra
ついかのおてつだいをして、うけとったおかね _____

☆ Celebrate WINS! / せいかのおいわいをしましょう!

I am proud of myself for
できて、ほこりにおもうこと _____

I went above and beyond by doing
いつもより、もっとがんばってやりとげたこと _____

My wish list
ほしいものリスト

I am saving my money for:
わたしがおかねをためているりゆう

	My wish list / ほしいものリスト	Price / きんがく
1 一		
2 二		
3 三		

Money Log
マネーログ

My wallet
わたしのさいふのなか

Starting balance
はじめのおかね _____

Date 月／日	Description ないよう	Money received はいったおかね	Money spent つかったおかね	Balance のこったおかね

How much I saved so far / いままでで、たまったおかね _____

My piggy bank savings
わたしのちょきんばこのなか

Starting balance:
はじめのおかね _____

Date 月／日	Description ないよう	Money received はいったおかね	Money spent つかったおかね	Balance のこったおかね

How much I saved so far / いままでで、たまったおかね _____

Week of / こんしゅうのひづけ _____

Goals for this week こんしゅうのもくひょう	☆ Chores to complete おてつだいをするかいすう _____	times かい
	☆ Money to earn: こんしゅう、うけとりたいおかね _____	

Chores おてつだいのないよう	S にち	M げつ	T か	W すい	T もく	F きん	S ど
1 一 _____	○	○	○	○	○	○	○
2 二 _____	○	○	○	○	○	○	○
3 三 _____	○	○	○	○	○	○	○
4 四 _____	○	○	○	○	○	○	○
5 五 _____	○	○	○	○	○	○	○

Memo
メモ

☆ Results / けっか

This week, I completed chores
こんしゅう、おてつだいができたかいすう _____ times かい

From my chores, I earned
おてつだいをして、うけとったおかね _____

From extra work, I earned extra
ついかのおてつだいをして、うけとったおかね _____

☆ Celebrate WINS! / せいかのおいわいをしましょう!

I am proud of myself for
できて、ほこりにおもうこと _____

I went above and beyond by doing
いつもより、もっとがんばってやりとげたこと _____

My wish list ほしいものリスト	I am saving my money for: わたしがおかねをためているりゆう	
	My wish list / ほしいものリスト	Price / きんがく
1 一		
2 二		
3 三		

Money Log
マネーログ

My wallet わたしのさいふのなか		Starting balance はじめのおかね _____		
Date 月／日	Description ないよう	Money received はいったおかね	Money spent つかったおかね	Balance のこったおかね

How much I saved so far / いままでで、たまったおかね _____

My piggy bank savings わたしのちょきんばこのなか		Starting balance: はじめのおかね _____		
Date 月／日	Description ないよう	Money received はいったおかね	Money spent つかったおかね	Balance のこったおかね

How much I saved so far / いままでで、たまったおかね _____

Week of / こんしゅうのひづけ _____

Goals for this week
こんしゅうのもくひょう

☆ Chores to complete   times
おてつだいをするかいすう _____ かい

☆ Money to earn:
こんしゅう、うけとりたいおかね _____

Chores / おてつだいのないよう	S にち	M げつ	T か	W すい	T もく	F きん	S ど
1 一 _____	○	○	○	○	○	○	○
2 二 _____	○	○	○	○	○	○	○
3 三 _____	○	○	○	○	○	○	○
4 四 _____	○	○	○	○	○	○	○
5 五 _____	○	○	○	○	○	○	○

Memo
メモ

☆ Results / けっか

This week, I completed chores   times
こんしゅう、おてつだいができたかいすう _____ かい

From my chores, I earned
おてつだいをして、うけとったおかね _____

From extra work, I earned extra
ついかのおてつだいをして、うけとったおかね _____

☆ Celebrate WINS! / せいかのおいわいをしましょう!

I am proud of myself for
できて、ほこりにおもうこと _____

I went above and beyond by doing
いつもより、もっとがんばってやりとげたこと _____

My wish list ほしいものリスト	I am saving my money for: わたしがおかねをためているりゆう	
	My wish list / ほしいものリスト	**Price / きんがく**
1 一		
2 二		
3 三		

Money Log
マネーログ

My wallet
わたしのさいふのなか

Starting balance
はじめのおかね _____

Date 月／日	Description ないよう	Money received はいったおかね	Money spent つかったおかね	Balance のこったおかね

How much I saved so far / いままでで、たまったおかね _____

My piggy bank savings
わたしのちょきんばこのなか

Starting balance:
はじめのおかね _____

Date 月／日	Description ないよう	Money received はいったおかね	Money spent つかったおかね	Balance のこったおかね

How much I saved so far / いままでで、たまったおかね _____

Week of / こんしゅうのひづけ _____

Goals for this week こんしゅうのもくひょう	☆ Chores to complete 　おてつだいをするかいすう _____	times かい
	☆ Money to earn: 　こんしゅう、うけとりたいおかね _____	

Chores おてつだいのないよう	S にち	M げつ	T か	W すい	T もく	F きん	S ど
1 一 _____	◯	◯	◯	◯	◯	◯	◯
2 二 _____	◯	◯	◯	◯	◯	◯	◯
3 三 _____	◯	◯	◯	◯	◯	◯	◯
4 四 _____	◯	◯	◯	◯	◯	◯	◯
5 五 _____	◯	◯	◯	◯	◯	◯	◯

Memo メモ

☆ Results / けっか

This week, I completed chores　　　　　　　　　　　　　　　　　　　　　times
こんしゅう、おてつだいができたかいすう _____ かい

From my chores, I earned
おてつだいをして、うけとったおかね _____

From extra work, I earned extra
ついかのおてつだいをして、うけとったおかね _____

☆ Celebrate WINS! / せいかのおいわいをしましょう!

I am proud of myself for
できて、ほこりにおもうこと _____

I went above and beyond by doing
いつもより、もっとがんばってやりとげたこと _____

My wish list ほしいものリスト	I am saving my money for: わたしがおかねをためているりゆう	
	My wish list / ほしいものリスト	**Price / きんがく**
1 一		
2 二		
3 三		

Money Log
マネーログ

My wallet
わたしのさいふのなか

Starting balance
はじめのおかね _____

Date 月／日	Description ないよう	Money received はいったおかね	Money spent つかったおかね	Balance のこったおかね

How much I saved so far / いままでで、たまったおかね _____

My piggy bank savings
わたしのちょきんばこのなか

Starting balance:
はじめのおかね _____

Date 月／日	Description ないよう	Money received はいったおかね	Money spent つかったおかね	Balance のこったおかね

How much I saved so far / いままでで、たまったおかね _____

Week of / こんしゅうのひづけ _____

Goals for this week こんしゅうのもくひょう	☆ Chores to complete おてつだいをするかいすう _____	times かい
	☆ Money to earn: こんしゅう、うけとりたいおかね _____	

Chores おてつだいのないよう	S にち	M げつ	T か	W すい	T もく	F きん	S ど
1 一 _____	◯	◯	◯	◯	◯	◯	◯
2 二 _____	◯	◯	◯	◯	◯	◯	◯
3 三 _____	◯	◯	◯	◯	◯	◯	◯
4 四 _____	◯	◯	◯	◯	◯	◯	◯
5 五 _____	◯	◯	◯	◯	◯	◯	◯

Memo
メモ

☆ Results / けっか

This week, I completed chores   times
こんしゅう、おてつだいができたかいすう _____ かい

From my chores, I earned
おてつだいをして、うけとったおかね _____

From extra work, I earned extra
ついかのおてつだいをして、うけとったおかね _____

☆ Celebrate WINS! / せいかのおいわいをしましょう!

I am proud of myself for
できて、ほこりにおもうこと _____

I went above and beyond by doing
いつもより、もっとがんばってやりとげたこと _____

My wish list
ほしいものリスト

I am saving my money for:
わたしがおかねをためているりゆう

	My wish list / ほしいものリスト	Price / きんがく
1 一		
2 二		
3 三		

Money Log
マネーログ

My wallet
わたしのさいふのなか

Starting balance
はじめのおかね _____

Date 月／日	Description ないよう	Money received はいったおかね	Money spent つかったおかね	Balance のこったおかね

How much I saved so far / いままでで、たまったおかね _____

My piggy bank savings
わたしのちょきんばこのなか

Starting balance:
はじめのおかね _____

Date 月／日	Description ないよう	Money received はいったおかね	Money spent つかったおかね	Balance のこったおかね

How much I saved so far / いままでで、たまったおかね _____

Week of / こんしゅうのひづけ _____

Goals for this week
こんしゅうのもくひょう

☆ Chores to complete   times
おてつだいをするかいすう _____ かい

☆ Money to earn:
こんしゅう、うけとりたいおかね _____

Chores おてつだいのないよう	S にち	M げつ	T か	W すい	T もく	F きん	S ど
1 一 _____	◯	◯	◯	◯	◯	◯	◯
2 二 _____	◯	◯	◯	◯	◯	◯	◯
3 三 _____	◯	◯	◯	◯	◯	◯	◯
4 四 _____	◯	◯	◯	◯	◯	◯	◯
5 五 _____	◯	◯	◯	◯	◯	◯	◯

Memo
メモ

☆ Results / けっか

This week, I completed chores   times
こんしゅう、おてつだいができたかいすう _____ かい

From my chores, I earned
おてつだいをして、うけとったおかね _____

From extra work, I earned extra
ついかのおてつだいをして、うけとったおかね _____

☆ Celebrate WINS! / せいかのおいわいをしましょう!

I am proud of myself for
できて、ほこりにおもうこと _____

I went above and beyond by doing
いつもより、もっとがんばってやりとげたこと _____

My wish list ほしいものリスト	I am saving my money for: わたしがおかねをためているりゆう	
	My wish list / ほしいものリスト	Price / きんがく
1 一		
2 二		
3 三		

Money Log
マネーログ

My wallet わたしのさいふのなか		Starting balance はじめのおかね _____		
Date 月／日	Description ないよう	Money received はいったおかね	Money spent つかったおかね	Balance のこったおかね

How much I saved so far / いままでで、たまったおかね _____

My piggy bank savings わたしのちょきんばこのなか		Starting balance: はじめのおかね _____		
Date 月／日	Description ないよう	Money received はいったおかね	Money spent つかったおかね	Balance のこったおかね

How much I saved so far / いままでで、たまったおかね _____

Week of / こんしゅうのひづけ _____

Goals for this week こんしゅうのもくひょう	☆ Chores to complete おてつだいをするかいすう _____	times かい
	☆ Money to earn: こんしゅう、うけとりたいおかね _____	

Chores おてつだいのないよう	S にち	M げつ	T か	W すい	T もく	F きん	S ど
1 一 _____	○	○	○	○	○	○	○
2 二 _____	○	○	○	○	○	○	○
3 三 _____	○	○	○	○	○	○	○
4 四 _____	○	○	○	○	○	○	○
5 五 _____	○	○	○	○	○	○	○

Memo
メモ

☆ Results / けっか

This week, I completed chores   times
こんしゅう、おてつだいができたかいすう _____ かい

From my chores, I earned
おてつだいをして、うけとったおかね _____

From extra work, I earned extra
ついかのおてつだいをして、うけとったおかね _____

☆ Celebrate WINS! / せいかのおいわいをしましょう!

I am proud of myself for
できて、ほこりにおもうこと _____

I went above and beyond by doing
いつもより、もっとがんばってやりとげたこと _____

My wish list
ほしいものリスト
I am saving my money for:
わたしがおかねをためているりゆう

	My wish list / ほしいものリスト	Price / きんがく
1 —		
2 二		
3 三		

Money Log
マネーログ

My wallet
わたしのさいふのなか
Starting balance
はじめのおかね _____

Date 月／日	Description ないよう	Money received はいったおかね	Money spent つかったおかね	Balance のこったおかね

How much I saved so far / いままでで、たまったおかね _____

My piggy bank savings
わたしのちょきんばこのなか
Starting balance:
はじめのおかね _____

Date 月／日	Description ないよう	Money received はいったおかね	Money spent つかったおかね	Balance のこったおかね

How much I saved so far / いままでで、たまったおかね _____

Week of / こんしゅうのひづけ _____

Goals for this week こんしゅうのもくひょう	☆ Chores to complete おてつだいをするかいすう _____	times かい
	☆ Money to earn: こんしゅう、うけとりたいおかね _____	

Chores おてつだいのないよう	S にち	M げつ	T か	W すい	T もく	F きん	S ど
1 一 _____	◯	◯	◯	◯	◯	◯	◯
2 二 _____	◯	◯	◯	◯	◯	◯	◯
3 三 _____	◯	◯	◯	◯	◯	◯	◯
4 四 _____	◯	◯	◯	◯	◯	◯	◯
5 五 _____	◯	◯	◯	◯	◯	◯	◯

Memo
メモ

☆ Results / けっか

This week, I completed chores
こんしゅう、おてつだいができたかいすう _____ times かい

From my chores, I earned
おてつだいをして、うけとったおかね _____

From extra work, I earned extra
ついかのおてつだいをして、うけとったおかね _____

☆ Celebrate WINS! / せいかのおいわいをしましょう!

I am proud of myself for
できて、ほこりにおもうこと _____

I went above and beyond by doing
いつもより、もっとがんばってやりとげたこと _____

My wish list ほしいものリスト	I am saving my money for: わたしがおかねをためているりゆう	
	My wish list / ほしいものリスト	Price / きんがく
1 一		
2 二		
3 三		

Money Log
マネーログ

My wallet
わたしのさいふのなか   Starting balance
はじめのおかね _____

Date 月／日	Description ないよう	Money received はいったおかね	Money spent つかったおかね	Balance のこったおかね

How much I saved so far / いままでで、たまったおかね _____

My piggy bank savings
わたしのちょきんばこのなか   Starting balance:
はじめのおかね _____

Date 月／日	Description ないよう	Money received はいったおかね	Money spent つかったおかね	Balance のこったおかね

How much I saved so far / いままでで、たまったおかね _____

Week of / こんしゅうのひづけ _____

Goals for this week こんしゅうのもくひょう	☆ Chores to complete おてつだいをするかいすう _____	times かい
	☆ Money to earn: こんしゅう、うけとりたいおかね _____	

Chores おてつだいのないよう	S にち	M げつ	T か	W すい	T もく	F きん	S ど
1 一 _____	◯	◯	◯	◯	◯	◯	◯
2 二 _____	◯	◯	◯	◯	◯	◯	◯
3 三 _____	◯	◯	◯	◯	◯	◯	◯
4 四 _____	◯	◯	◯	◯	◯	◯	◯
5 五 _____	◯	◯	◯	◯	◯	◯	◯

Memo
メモ

☆ Results / けっか

This week, I completed chores   times
こんしゅう、おてつだいができたかいすう _____ かい

From my chores, I earned
おてつだいをして、うけとったおかね _____

From extra work, I earned extra
ついかのおてつだいをして、うけとったおかね _____

☆ Celebrate WINS! / せいかのおいわいをしましょう!

I am proud of myself for
できて、ほこりにおもうこと _____

I went above and beyond by doing
いつもより、もっとがんばってやりとげたこと _____

My wish list ほしいものリスト	I am saving my money for: わたしがおかねをためているりゆう	
	My wish list / ほしいものリスト	Price / きんがく
1 一		
2 二		
3 三		

Money Log
マネーログ

My wallet わたしのさいふのなか		Starting balance はじめのおかね _____		
Date 月／日	Description ないよう	Money received はいったおかね	Money spent つかったおかね	Balance のこったおかね

How much I saved so far / いままでで、たまったおかね _____

My piggy bank savings わたしのちょきんばこのなか		Starting balance: はじめのおかね _____		
Date 月／日	Description ないよう	Money received はいったおかね	Money spent つかったおかね	Balance のこったおかね

How much I saved so far / いままでで、たまったおかね _____

Week of / こんしゅうのひづけ _____

Goals for this week こんしゅうのもくひょう	☆ Chores to complete おてつだいをするかいすう _____	times かい
	☆ Money to earn: こんしゅう、うけとりたいおかね _____	

Chores おてつだいのないよう	S にち	M げつ	T か	W すい	T もく	F きん	S ど
1 一 _____	◯	◯	◯	◯	◯	◯	◯
2 二 _____	◯	◯	◯	◯	◯	◯	◯
3 三 _____	◯	◯	◯	◯	◯	◯	◯
4 四 _____	◯	◯	◯	◯	◯	◯	◯
5 五 _____	◯	◯	◯	◯	◯	◯	◯

Memo
メモ

☆ Results / けっか

This week, I completed chores   times
こんしゅう、おてつだいができたかいすう _____ かい

From my chores, I earned
おてつだいをして、うけとったおかね _____

From extra work, I earned extra
ついかのおてつだいをして、うけとったおかね _____

☆ Celebrate WINS! / せいかのおいわいをしましょう!

I am proud of myself for
できて、ほこりにおもうこと _____

I went above and beyond by doing
いつもより、もっとがんばってやりとげたこと _____

My wish list ほしいものリスト	I am saving my money for: わたしがおかねをためているりゆう	
	My wish list / ほしいものリスト	Price / きんがく
1 一		
2 二		
3 三		

Money Log
マネーログ

My wallet わたしのさいふのなか		Starting balance はじめのおかね _____		
Date 月／日	Description ないよう	Money received はいったおかね	Money spent つかったおかね	Balance のこったおかね

How much I saved so far / いままでで、たまったおかね _____

My piggy bank savings わたしのちょきんばこのなか		Starting balance: はじめのおかね _____		
Date 月／日	Description ないよう	Money received はいったおかね	Money spent つかったおかね	Balance のこったおかね

How much I saved so far / いままでで、たまったおかね _____

Week of / こんしゅうのひづけ _____

Goals for this week こんしゅうのもくひょう	☆ Chores to complete おてつだいをするかいすう _____	times かい
	☆ Money to earn: こんしゅう、うけとりたいおかね _____	

Chores おてつだいのないよう	S にち	M げつ	T か	W すい	T もく	F きん	S ど
1 一 _____	○	○	○	○	○	○	○
2 二 _____	○	○	○	○	○	○	○
3 三 _____	○	○	○	○	○	○	○
4 四 _____	○	○	○	○	○	○	○
5 五 _____	○	○	○	○	○	○	○

Memo
メモ

☆ Results / けっか

This week, I completed chores
こんしゅう、おてつだいができたかいすう _____ times かい

From my chores, I earned
おてつだいをして、うけとったおかね _____

From extra work, I earned extra
ついかのおてつだいをして、うけとったおかね _____

☆ Celebrate WINS! / せいかのおいわいをしましょう!

I am proud of myself for
できて、ほこりにおもうこと _____

I went above and beyond by doing
いつもより、もっとがんばってやりとげたこと _____

My wish list ほしいものリスト	I am saving my money for: わたしがおかねをためているりゆう	
	My wish list / ほしいものリスト	Price / きんがく
1 一		
2 二		
3 三		

Money Log
マネーログ

My wallet
わたしのさいふのなか　　　　　　Starting balance
　　　　　　　　　　　　　　　　はじめのおかね ＿＿＿＿＿＿＿＿＿＿

Date 月／日	Description ないよう	Money received はいったおかね	Money spent つかったおかね	Balance のこったおかね

How much I saved so far / いままでで、たまったおかね ＿＿＿＿＿＿＿＿＿＿

My piggy bank savings
わたしのちょきんばこのなか　　　　Starting balance:
　　　　　　　　　　　　　　　　はじめのおかね ＿＿＿＿＿＿＿＿＿＿

Date 月／日	Description ないよう	Money received はいったおかね	Money spent つかったおかね	Balance のこったおかね

How much I saved so far / いままでで、たまったおかね ＿＿＿＿＿＿＿＿＿＿

Week of / こんしゅうのひづけ _____

Goals for this week
こんしゅうのもくひょう

☆ Chores to complete　　　　　　　　　　　　　times
　おてつだいをするかいすう _____ かい
☆ Money to earn:
　こんしゅう、うけとりたいおかね _____

Chores おてつだいのないよう	S にち	M げつ	T か	W すい	T もく	F きん	S ど
1 一 _____	◯	◯	◯	◯	◯	◯	◯
2 二 _____	◯	◯	◯	◯	◯	◯	◯
3 三 _____	◯	◯	◯	◯	◯	◯	◯
4 四 _____	◯	◯	◯	◯	◯	◯	◯
5 五 _____	◯	◯	◯	◯	◯	◯	◯

Memo
メモ

☆ Results / けっか

This week, I completed chores　　　　　　　　　　　　　　　times
こんしゅう、おてつだいができたかいすう _____ かい

From my chores, I earned
おてつだいをして、うけとったおかね _____

From extra work, I earned extra
ついかのおてつだいをして、うけとったおかね _____

☆ Celebrate WINS! / せいかのおいわいをしましょう!

I am proud of myself for
できて、ほこりにおもうこと _____

I went above and beyond by doing
いつもより、もっとがんばってやりとげたこと _____

My wish list
ほしいものリスト
I am saving my money for:
わたしがおかねをためているりゆう

	My wish list / ほしいものリスト	Price / きんがく
1 一		
2 二		
3 三		

Money Log
マネーログ

My wallet
わたしのさいふのなか

Starting balance
はじめのおかね _____

Date 月／日	Description ないよう	Money received はいったおかね	Money spent つかったおかね	Balance のこったおかね

How much I saved so far / いままでで、たまったおかね _____

My piggy bank savings
わたしのちょきんばこのなか

Starting balance:
はじめのおかね _____

Date 月／日	Description ないよう	Money received はいったおかね	Money spent つかったおかね	Balance のこったおかね

How much I saved so far / いままでで、たまったおかね _____

Week of / こんしゅうのひづけ _____

Goals for this week こんしゅうのもくひょう	☆ Chores to complete おてつだいをするかいすう _____	times かい
	☆ Money to earn: こんしゅう、うけとりたいおかね _____	

Chores おてつだいのないよう	S にち	M げつ	T か	W すい	T もく	F きん	S ど
1 一 _____	○	○	○	○	○	○	○
2 二 _____	○	○	○	○	○	○	○
3 三 _____	○	○	○	○	○	○	○
4 四 _____	○	○	○	○	○	○	○
5 五 _____	○	○	○	○	○	○	○

Memo
メモ

☆ Results / けっか

This week, I completed chores   times
こんしゅう、おてつだいができたかいすう _____ かい

From my chores, I earned
おてつだいをして、うけとったおかね _____

From extra work, I earned extra
ついかのおてつだいをして、うけとったおかね _____

☆ Celebrate WINS! / せいかのおいわいをしましょう!

I am proud of myself for
できて、ほこりにおもうこと _____

I went above and beyond by doing
いつもより、もっとがんばってやりとげたこと _____

My wish list ほしいものリスト	I am saving my money for: わたしがおかねをためているりゆう	
	My wish list / ほしいものリスト	**Price / きんがく**
1 一		
2 二		
3 三		

Money Log
マネーログ

My wallet わたしのさいふのなか		Starting balance はじめのおかね ＿＿＿＿＿＿		
Date 月／日	**Description ないよう**	**Money received はいったおかね**	**Money spent つかったおかね**	**Balance のこったおかね**

How much I saved so far / いままでで、たまったおかね ＿＿＿＿＿＿

My piggy bank savings わたしのちょきんばこのなか		Starting balance: はじめのおかね ＿＿＿＿＿＿		
Date 月／日	**Description ないよう**	**Money received はいったおかね**	**Money spent つかったおかね**	**Balance のこったおかね**

How much I saved so far / いままでで、たまったおかね ＿＿＿＿＿＿

Week of / こんしゅうのひづけ _____

Goals for this week こんしゅうのもくひょう	☆ Chores to complete おてつだいをするかいすう _____	times かい
	☆ Money to earn: こんしゅう、うけとりたいおかね _____	

Chores おてつだいのないよう	S にち	M げつ	T か	W すい	T もく	F きん	S ど
1 一 _____	○	○	○	○	○	○	○
2 二 _____	○	○	○	○	○	○	○
3 三 _____	○	○	○	○	○	○	○
4 四 _____	○	○	○	○	○	○	○
5 五 _____	○	○	○	○	○	○	○

Memo
メモ

☆ Results / けっか

This week, I completed chores   times
こんしゅう、おてつだいができたかいすう _____ かい

From my chores, I earned
おてつだいをして、うけとったおかね _____

From extra work, I earned extra
ついかのおてつだいをして、うけとったおかね _____

☆ Celebrate WINS! / せいかのおいわいをしましょう!

I am proud of myself for
できて、ほこりにおもうこと _____
I went above and beyond by doing
いつもより、もっとがんばってやりとげたこと _____

My wish list ほしいものリスト	I am saving my money for: わたしがおかねをためているりゆう	
	My wish list / ほしいものリスト	Price / きんがく
1 一		
2 二		
3 三		

Money Log
マネーログ

My wallet
わたしのさいふのなか   **Starting balance**
                           はじめのおかね _____

Date 月／日	Description ないよう	Money received はいったおかね	Money spent つかったおかね	Balance のこったおかね

How much I saved so far / いままでで、たまったおかね _____

My piggy bank savings
わたしのちょきんばこのなか   **Starting balance:**
                              はじめのおかね _____

Date 月／日	Description ないよう	Money received はいったおかね	Money spent つかったおかね	Balance のこったおかね

How much I saved so far / いままでで、たまったおかね _____

Week of / こんしゅうのひづけ _____

Goals for this week
こんしゅうのもくひょう

☆ **Chores to complete**   times
おてつだいをするかいすう _____ かい

☆ **Money to earn:**
こんしゅう、うけとりたいおかね _____

Chores おてつだいのないよう	S にち	M げつ	T か	W すい	T もく	F きん	S ど
1 一 _____	○	○	○	○	○	○	○
2 二 _____	○	○	○	○	○	○	○
3 三 _____	○	○	○	○	○	○	○
4 四 _____	○	○	○	○	○	○	○
5 五 _____	○	○	○	○	○	○	○

Memo
メモ

☆ Results / けっか

This week, I completed chores   times
こんしゅう、おてつだいができたかいすう _____ かい

From my chores, I earned
おてつだいをして、うけとったおかね _____

From extra work, I earned extra
ついかのおてつだいをして、うけとったおかね _____

☆ Celebrate WINS! / せいかのおいわいをしましょう!

I am proud of myself for
できて、ほこりにおもうこと _____

I went above and beyond by doing
いつもより、もっとがんばってやりとげたこと _____

My wish list ほしいものリスト	I am saving my money for: わたしがおかねをためているりゆう	
	My wish list / ほしいものリスト	Price / きんがく
1 一		
2 二		
3 三		

Money Log
マネーログ

My wallet わたしのさいふのなか		Starting balance はじめのおかね _____		
Date 月／日	Description ないよう	Money received はいったおかね	Money spent つかったおかね	Balance のこったおかね

How much I saved so far / いままでで、たまったおかね _____

My piggy bank savings わたしのちょきんばこのなか		Starting balance: はじめのおかね _____		
Date 月／日	Description ないよう	Money received はいったおかね	Money spent つかったおかね	Balance のこったおかね

How much I saved so far / いままでで、たまったおかね _____

Week of / こんしゅうのひづけ _____

| Goals for this week こんしゅうのもくひょう | ☆ Chores to complete おてつだいをするかいすう _____ times かい |
| | ☆ Money to earn: こんしゅう、うけとりたいおかね _____ |

Chores おてつだいのないよう	S にち	M げつ	T か	W すい	T もく	F きん	S ど
1 一 _____	○	○	○	○	○	○	○
2 二 _____	○	○	○	○	○	○	○
3 三 _____	○	○	○	○	○	○	○
4 四 _____	○	○	○	○	○	○	○
5 五 _____	○	○	○	○	○	○	○

Memo
メモ

☆ Results / けっか

This week, I completed chores
こんしゅう、おてつだいができたかいすう _____ times かい

From my chores, I earned
おてつだいをして、うけとったおかね _____

From extra work, I earned extra
ついかのおてつだいをして、うけとったおかね _____

☆ Celebrate WINS! / せいかのおいわいをしましょう!

I am proud of myself for
できて、ほこりにおもうこと _____

I went above and beyond by doing
いつもより、もっとがんばってやりとげたこと _____

My wish list ほしいものリスト I am saving my money for: わたしがおかねをためているりゆう		
	My wish list / ほしいものリスト	Price / きんがく
1 一		
2 二		
3 三		

Money Log
マネーログ

My wallet
わたしのさいふのなか

Starting balance
はじめのおかね _____

Date 月／日	Description ないよう	Money received はいったおかね	Money spent つかったおかね	Balance のこったおかね

How much I saved so far / いままでで、たまったおかね _____

My piggy bank savings
わたしのちょきんばこのなか

Starting balance:
はじめのおかね _____

Date 月／日	Description ないよう	Money received はいったおかね	Money spent つかったおかね	Balance のこったおかね

How much I saved so far / いままでで、たまったおかね _____

Week of / こんしゅうのひづけ _____

Goals for this week こんしゅうのもくひょう	☆ **Chores to complete**　　　　　　　**times** 　おてつだいをするかいすう _____ かい ☆ **Money to earn:** 　こんしゅう、うけとりたいおかね _____

Chores おてつだいのないよう	S にち	M げつ	T か	W すい	T もく	F きん	S ど
1 一 _____	○	○	○	○	○	○	○
2 二 _____	○	○	○	○	○	○	○
3 三 _____	○	○	○	○	○	○	○
4 四 _____	○	○	○	○	○	○	○
5 五 _____	○	○	○	○	○	○	○

Memo
メモ

☆ Results / けっか

This week, I completed chores　　　　　　　　　　　　　　　　**times**
こんしゅう、おてつだいができたかいすう _____ かい

From my chores, I earned
おてつだいをして、うけとったおかね _____

From extra work, I earned extra
ついかのおてつだいをして、うけとったおかね _____

☆ Celebrate WINS! / せいかのおいわいをしましょう!

I am proud of myself for
できて、ほこりにおもうこと _____

I went above and beyond by doing
いつもより、もっとがんばってやりとげたこと _____

My wish list ほしいものリスト	I am saving my money for: わたしがおかねをためているりゆう	
	My wish list / ほしいものリスト	Price / きんがく
1 一		
2 二		
3 三		

Money Log
マネーログ

My wallet
わたしのさいふのなか　　　　　　　　Starting balance
　　　　　　　　　　　　　　　　はじめのおかね _____

Date 月／日	Description ないよう	Money received はいったおかね	Money spent つかったおかね	Balance のこったおかね

How much I saved so far / いままでで、たまったおかね _____

My piggy bank savings
わたしのちょきんばこのなか　　　　　Starting balance:
　　　　　　　　　　　　　　　　はじめのおかね _____

Date 月／日	Description ないよう	Money received はいったおかね	Money spent つかったおかね	Balance のこったおかね

How much I saved so far / いままでで、たまったおかね _____

Week of / こんしゅうのひづけ _____

Goals for this week こんしゅうのもくひょう	☆ Chores to complete おてつだいをするかいすう _____	times かい
	☆ Money to earn: こんしゅう、うけとりたいおかね _____	

Chores おてつだいのないよう	S にち	M げつ	T か	W すい	T もく	F きん	S ど
1 一 _____	○	○	○	○	○	○	○
2 二 _____	○	○	○	○	○	○	○
3 三 _____	○	○	○	○	○	○	○
4 四 _____	○	○	○	○	○	○	○
5 五 _____	○	○	○	○	○	○	○

Memo
メモ

☆ Results / けっか

This week, I completed chores
こんしゅう、おてつだいができたかいすう _____ times かい

From my chores, I earned
おてつだいをして、うけとったおかね _____

From extra work, I earned extra
ついかのおてつだいをして、うけとったおかね _____

☆ Celebrate WINS! / せいかのおいわいをしましょう!

I am proud of myself for
できて、ほこりにおもうこと _____

I went above and beyond by doing
いつもより、もっとがんばってやりとげたこと _____

My wish list ほしいものリスト	I am saving my money for: わたしがおかねをためているりゆう	
	My wish list / ほしいものリスト	Price / きんがく
1 一		
2 二		
3 三		

Money Log
マネーログ

My wallet
わたしのさいふのなか

Starting balance
はじめのおかね _____

Date 月／日	Description ないよう	Money received はいったおかね	Money spent つかったおかね	Balance のこったおかね

How much I saved so far / いままでで、たまったおかね _____

My piggy bank savings
わたしのちょきんばこのなか

Starting balance:
はじめのおかね _____

Date 月／日	Description ないよう	Money received はいったおかね	Money spent つかったおかね	Balance のこったおかね

How much I saved so far / いままでで、たまったおかね _____

Week of / こんしゅうのひづけ _____

Goals for this week こんしゅうのもくひょう	☆ Chores to complete おてつだいをするかいすう _____	times かい
	☆ Money to earn: こんしゅう、うけとりたいおかね _____	

Chores おてつだいのないよう	S にち	M げつ	T か	W すい	T もく	F きん	S ど
1 一 _____	○	○	○	○	○	○	○
2 二 _____	○	○	○	○	○	○	○
3 三 _____	○	○	○	○	○	○	○
4 四 _____	○	○	○	○	○	○	○
5 五 _____	○	○	○	○	○	○	○

Memo
メモ

☆ Results / けっか

This week, I completed chores   times
こんしゅう、おてつだいができたかいすう _____ かい

From my chores, I earned
おてつだいをして、うけとったおかね _____

From extra work, I earned extra
ついかのおてつだいをして、うけとったおかね _____

☆ Celebrate WINS! / せいかのおいわいをしましょう!

I am proud of myself for
できて、ほこりにおもうこと _____

I went above and beyond by doing
いつもより、もっとがんばってやりとげたこと _____

My wish list ほしいものリスト	I am saving my money for: わたしがおかねをためているりゆう	
	My wish list / ほしいものリスト	Price / きんがく
1 一		
2 二		
3 三		

Money Log
マネーログ

My wallet わたしのさいふのなか		Starting balance はじめのおかね _____		
Date 月／日	Description ないよう	Money received はいったおかね	Money spent つかったおかね	Balance のこったおかね

How much I saved so far / いままでで、たまったおかね _____

My piggy bank savings わたしのちょきんばこのなか		Starting balance: はじめのおかね _____		
Date 月／日	Description ないよう	Money received はいったおかね	Money spent つかったおかね	Balance のこったおかね

How much I saved so far / いままでで、たまったおかね _____

Week of / こんしゅうのひづけ _____

Goals for this week こんしゅうのもくひょう	☆ Chores to complete おてつだいをするかいすう _____	times かい
	☆ Money to earn: こんしゅう、うけとりたいおかね _____	

Chores おてつだいのないよう	S にち	M げつ	T か	W すい	T もく	F きん	S ど
1 一 _____	○	○	○	○	○	○	○
2 二 _____	○	○	○	○	○	○	○
3 三 _____	○	○	○	○	○	○	○
4 四 _____	○	○	○	○	○	○	○
5 五 _____	○	○	○	○	○	○	○

Memo
メモ

☆ Results / けっか

This week, I completed chores
こんしゅう、おてつだいができたかいすう _____ times かい

From my chores, I earned
おてつだいをして、うけとったおかね _____

From extra work, I earned extra
ついかのおてつだいをして、うけとったおかね _____

☆ Celebrate WINS! / せいかのおいわいをしましょう!

I am proud of myself for
できて、ほこりにおもうこと _____

I went above and beyond by doing
いつもより、もっとがんばってやりとげたこと _____

My wish list ほしいものリスト	I am saving my money for: わたしがおかねをためているりゆう	

	My wish list / ほしいものリスト	Price / きんがく
1 一		
2 二		
3 三		

 # Money Log
マネーログ

My wallet わたしのさいふのなか		Starting balance はじめのおかね _____		
Date 月／日	Description ないよう	Money received はいったおかね	Money spent つかったおかね	Balance のこったおかね

How much I saved so far / いままでで、たまったおかね _____

My piggy bank savings わたしのちょきんばこのなか		Starting balance: はじめのおかね _____		
Date 月／日	Description ないよう	Money received はいったおかね	Money spent つかったおかね	Balance のこったおかね

How much I saved so far / いままでで、たまったおかね _____

Week of / こんしゅうのひづけ _____

Goals for this week
こんしゅうのもくひょう

☆ Chores to complete   times
おてつだいをするかいすう _____ かい
☆ Money to earn:
こんしゅう、うけとりたいおかね _____

Chores おてつだいのないよう	S にち	M げつ	T か	W すい	T もく	F きん	S ど
1 一 _____	○	○	○	○	○	○	○
2 二 _____	○	○	○	○	○	○	○
3 三 _____	○	○	○	○	○	○	○
4 四 _____	○	○	○	○	○	○	○
5 五 _____	○	○	○	○	○	○	○

Memo
メモ

☆ Results / けっか

This week, I completed chores   times
こんしゅう、おてつだいができたかいすう _____ かい

From my chores, I earned
おてつだいをして、うけとったおかね _____

From extra work, I earned extra
ついかのおてつだいをして、うけとったおかね _____

☆ Celebrate WINS! / せいかのおいわいをしましょう!

I am proud of myself for
できて、ほこりにおもうこと _____

I went above and beyond by doing
いつもより、もっとがんばってやりとげたこと _____

My wish list ほしいものリスト	I am saving my money for: わたしがおかねをためているりゆう	
	My wish list / ほしいものリスト	Price / きんがく
1 一		
2 二		
3 三		

Money Log
マネーログ

My wallet わたしのさいふのなか		Starting balance はじめのおかね _____		
Date 月／日	Description ないよう	Money received はいったおかね	Money spent つかったおかね	Balance のこったおかね

How much I saved so far / いままでで、たまったおかね _____

My piggy bank savings わたしのちょきんばこのなか		Starting balance: はじめのおかね _____		
Date 月／日	Description ないよう	Money received はいったおかね	Money spent つかったおかね	Balance のこったおかね

How much I saved so far / いままでで、たまったおかね _____

Week of / こんしゅうのひづけ _____

Goals for this week こんしゅうのもくひょう	☆ Chores to complete おてつだいをするかいすう _____	times かい
	☆ Money to earn: こんしゅう、うけとりたいおかね _____	

Chores おてつだいのないよう	S にち	M げつ	T か	W すい	T もく	F きん	S ど
1 一 _____	○	○	○	○	○	○	○
2 二 _____	○	○	○	○	○	○	○
3 三 _____	○	○	○	○	○	○	○
4 四 _____	○	○	○	○	○	○	○
5 五 _____	○	○	○	○	○	○	○

Memo
メモ

☆ Results / けっか

This week, I completed chores   times
こんしゅう、おてつだいができたかいすう _____ かい

From my chores, I earned
おてつだいをして、うけとったおかね _____

From extra work, I earned extra
ついかのおてつだいをして、うけとったおかね _____

☆ Celebrate WINS! / せいかのおいわいをしましょう!

I am proud of myself for
できて、ほこりにおもうこと _____

I went above and beyond by doing
いつもより、もっとがんばってやりとげたこと _____

My wish list ほしいものリスト	I am saving my money for: わたしがおかねをためているりゆう	
	My wish list / ほしいものリスト	Price / きんがく
1 一		
2 二		
3 三		

Money Log
マネーログ

My wallet
わたしのさいふのなか   Starting balance
                             はじめのおかね _____

Date 月／日	Description ないよう	Money received はいったおかね	Money spent つかったおかね	Balance のこったおかね

How much I saved so far / いままでで、たまったおかね _____

My piggy bank savings
わたしのちょきんばこのなか   Starting balance:
                                   はじめのおかね _____

Date 月／日	Description ないよう	Money received はいったおかね	Money spent つかったおかね	Balance のこったおかね

How much I saved so far / いままでで、たまったおかね _____

Week of / こんしゅうのひづけ _____

Goals for this week
こんしゅうのもくひょう

☆ Chores to complete   times
   おてつだいをするかいすう _____ かい
☆ Money to earn:
   こんしゅう、うけとりたいおかね _____

Chores おてつだいのないよう	S にち	M げつ	T か	W すい	T もく	F きん	S ど
1 一 _____	◯	◯	◯	◯	◯	◯	◯
2 二 _____	◯	◯	◯	◯	◯	◯	◯
3 三 _____	◯	◯	◯	◯	◯	◯	◯
4 四 _____	◯	◯	◯	◯	◯	◯	◯
5 五 _____	◯	◯	◯	◯	◯	◯	◯

Memo
メモ

☆ Results / けっか

This week, I completed chores   times
こんしゅう、おてつだいができたかいすう _____ かい

From my chores, I earned
おてつだいをして、うけとったおかね _____

From extra work, I earned extra
ついかのおてつだいをして、うけとったおかね _____

☆ Celebrate WINS! / せいかのおいわいをしましょう!

I am proud of myself for
できて、ほこりにおもうこと _____

I went above and beyond by doing
いつもより、もっとがんばってやりとげたこと _____

My wish list ほしいものリスト	I am saving my money for: わたしがおかねをためているりゆう	
	My wish list / ほしいものリスト	**Price / きんがく**
1 一		
2 二		
3 三		

 # Money Log マネーログ

My wallet わたしのさいふのなか		Starting balance はじめのおかね _____		
Date 月／日	**Description ないよう**	**Money received はいったおかね**	**Money spent つかったおかね**	**Balance のこったおかね**

How much I saved so far / いままでで、たまったおかね _____

My piggy bank savings わたしのちょきんばこのなか		Starting balance: はじめのおかね _____		
Date 月／日	**Description ないよう**	**Money received はいったおかね**	**Money spent つかったおかね**	**Balance のこったおかね**

How much I saved so far / いままでで、たまったおかね _____

Week of / こんしゅうのひづけ _____

Goals for this week
こんしゅうのもくひょう

☆ **Chores to complete**   **times**
おてつだいをするかいすう _____ かい

☆ **Money to earn:**
こんしゅう、うけとりたいおかね _____

Chores おてつだいのないよう	S にち	M げつ	T か	W すい	T もく	F きん	S ど
1 一 _____	○	○	○	○	○	○	○
2 二 _____	○	○	○	○	○	○	○
3 三 _____	○	○	○	○	○	○	○
4 四 _____	○	○	○	○	○	○	○
5 五 _____	○	○	○	○	○	○	○

Memo
メモ

☆ Results / けっか

This week, I completed chores   **times**
こんしゅう、おてつだいができたかいすう _____ かい

From my chores, I earned
おてつだいをして、うけとったおかね _____

From extra work, I earned extra
ついかのおてつだいをして、うけとったおかね _____

☆ Celebrate WINS! / せいかのおいわいをしましょう!

I am proud of myself for
できて、ほこりにおもうこと _____

I went above and beyond by doing
いつもより、もっとがんばってやりとげたこと _____

My wish list ほしいものリスト	I am saving my money for: わたしがおかねをためているりゆう		
	My wish list / ほしいものリスト		Price / きんがく
1 一			
2 二			
3 三			

 # Money Log
マネーログ

My wallet
わたしのさいふのなか

Starting balance
はじめのおかね _____

Date 月／日	Description ないよう	Money received はいったおかね	Money spent つかったおかね	Balance のこったおかね

How much I saved so far / いままでで、たまったおかね _____

My piggy bank savings
わたしのちょきんばこのなか

Starting balance:
はじめのおかね _____

Date 月／日	Description ないよう	Money received はいったおかね	Money spent つかったおかね	Balance のこったおかね

How much I saved so far / いままでで、たまったおかね _____

Week of / こんしゅうのひづけ _____

Goals for this week
こんしゅうのもくひょう

☆ Chores to complete
おてつだいをするかいすう _____ かい   times

☆ Money to earn:
こんしゅう、うけとりたいおかね _____

Chores おてつだいのないよう	S にち	M げつ	T か	W すい	T もく	F きん	S ど
1 一 _____	○	○	○	○	○	○	○
2 二 _____	○	○	○	○	○	○	○
3 三 _____	○	○	○	○	○	○	○
4 四 _____	○	○	○	○	○	○	○
5 五 _____	○	○	○	○	○	○	○

Memo
メモ

☆ Results / けっか

This week, I completed chores   times
こんしゅう、おてつだいができたかいすう _____ かい

From my chores, I earned
おてつだいをして、うけとったおかね _____

From extra work, I earned extra
ついかのおてつだいをして、うけとったおかね _____

☆ Celebrate WINS! / せいかのおいわいをしましょう!

I am proud of myself for
できて、ほこりにおもうこと _____

I went above and beyond by doing
いつもより、もっとがんばってやりとげたこと _____

	My wish list / ほしいものリスト	Price / きんがく
1 一		
2 二		
3 三		

My wish list
ほしいものリスト

I am saving my money for:
わたしがおかねをためているりゆう

Money Log
マネーログ

My wallet
わたしのさいふのなか

Starting balance
はじめのおかね _____

Date 月／日	Description ないよう	Money received はいったおかね	Money spent つかったおかね	Balance のこったおかね

How much I saved so far / いままでで、たまったおかね _____

My piggy bank savings
わたしのちょきんばこのなか

Starting balance:
はじめのおかね _____

Date 月／日	Description ないよう	Money received はいったおかね	Money spent つかったおかね	Balance のこったおかね

How much I saved so far / いままでで、たまったおかね _____

Week of / こんしゅうのひづけ _____

Goals for this week こんしゅうのもくひょう	☆ Chores to complete おてつだいをするかいすう _____	times かい
	☆ Money to earn: こんしゅう、うけとりたいおかね _____	

Chores おてつだいのないよう	S にち	M げつ	T か	W すい	T もく	F きん	S ど
1 一 _____	○	○	○	○	○	○	○
2 二 _____	○	○	○	○	○	○	○
3 三 _____	○	○	○	○	○	○	○
4 四 _____	○	○	○	○	○	○	○
5 五 _____	○	○	○	○	○	○	○

Memo
メモ

☆ Results / けっか

This week, I completed chores
こんしゅう、おてつだいができたかいすう _____ times かい

From my chores, I earned
おてつだいをして、うけとったおかね _____

From extra work, I earned extra
ついかのおてつだいをして、うけとったおかね _____

☆ Celebrate WINS! / せいかのおいわいをしましょう!

I am proud of myself for
できて、ほこりにおもうこと _____

I went above and beyond by doing
いつもより、もっとがんばってやりとげたこと _____

My wish list ほしいものリスト	I am saving my money for: わたしがおかねをためているりゆう	
	My wish list / ほしいものリスト	**Price / きんがく**
1 一		
2 二		
3 三		

Money Log
マネーログ

My wallet わたしのさいふのなか		Starting balance はじめのおかね _____		
Date 月／日	**Description** ないよう	**Money received** はいったおかね	**Money spent** つかったおかね	**Balance** のこったおかね

How much I saved so far / いままでで、たまったおかね _____

My piggy bank savings わたしのちょきんばこのなか		Starting balance: はじめのおかね _____		
Date 月／日	**Description** ないよう	**Money received** はいったおかね	**Money spent** つかったおかね	**Balance** のこったおかね

How much I saved so far / いままでで、たまったおかね _____

Week of / こんしゅうのひづけ _____

Goals for this week
こんしゅうのもくひょう

☆ Chores to complete   times
おてつだいをするかいすう _____ かい

☆ Money to earn:
こんしゅう、うけとりたいおかね _____

Chores おてつだいのないよう	S にち	M げつ	T か	W すい	T もく	F きん	S ど
1 一 _____	◯	◯	◯	◯	◯	◯	◯
2 二 _____	◯	◯	◯	◯	◯	◯	◯
3 三 _____	◯	◯	◯	◯	◯	◯	◯
4 四 _____	◯	◯	◯	◯	◯	◯	◯
5 五 _____	◯	◯	◯	◯	◯	◯	◯

Memo
メモ

☆ Results / けっか

This week, I completed chores   times
こんしゅう、おてつだいができたかいすう _____ かい

From my chores, I earned
おてつだいをして、うけとったおかね _____

From extra work, I earned extra
ついかのおてつだいをして、うけとったおかね _____

☆ Celebrate WINS! / せいかのおいわいをしましょう!

I am proud of myself for
できて、ほこりにおもうこと _____

I went above and beyond by doing
いつもより、もっとがんばってやりとげたこと _____

My wish list ほしいものリスト	I am saving my money for: わたしがおかねをためているりゆう	
	My wish list / ほしいものリスト	Price / きんがく
1 一		
2 二		
3 三		

Money Log
マネーログ

My wallet
わたしのさいふのなか

Starting balance
はじめのおかね _____

Date 月／日	Description ないよう	Money received はいったおかね	Money spent つかったおかね	Balance のこったおかね

How much I saved so far / いままでで、たまったおかね _____

My piggy bank savings
わたしのちょきんばこのなか

Starting balance:
はじめのおかね _____

Date 月／日	Description ないよう	Money received はいったおかね	Money spent つかったおかね	Balance のこったおかね

How much I saved so far / いままでで、たまったおかね _____

ONE YEAR PROGRESS

<ruby>一<rt>いち</rt>年<rt>ねん</rt></ruby> の <ruby>進<rt>しん</rt> 捗<rt>ちょく</rt></ruby>

My wallet わたしのさいふのなか

Starting balance noted on page 19

19 ページにかいた、はじめのおかね _____

Ending balance noted on page 121

121 ページにかいた、いままでで、たまったおかね _____

How much I saved in a year (52 weeks)

いちねん(52 しゅうかん)で、ためたおかね _____

My piggy bank savings わたしのちょきんばこのなか

Starting balance noted on page 19

19 ページにかいた、はじめのおかね _____

Ending balance noted on page 121

121 ページにかいた、いままでで、たまったおかね _____

How much I saved in a year (52 weeks)

いちねん(52 しゅうかん)で、ためたおかね _____

You did it! Great job!

やったね！がんばったね！

122

Made in the USA
Columbia, SC
05 May 2023

16150050R00070